Programming the SIMPL Way

John Collins   Robert Findlay

ISBN 978-0-557-01270-1

Dedicated to Dan Hildebrand

A deep thinker and a really nice guy who was taken from us too soon.

Contents

III   SIMPL Toolkit   93

8   Testing Framework   95

9   SIMPL Sandbox   107

IV   SIMPL Example Project   111

10 A SIMPL Project - Putting It All Together   113

11 Test Plan   119

12 Directory Tree   125

List of Figures

List of Tables

Preface

The theme of this book is really the story of a software journey. Because this journey has been undertaken by real people, we hope that it serves to put a human face on the subject. This a book about SIMPL. SIMPL, at its most basic level is a library of functions that enable two or more software programs to communicate with each other by sending and receiving information in the form of enclosed messages. SIMPL modules can be many things. They are great containers for encapsulating complexity in a software algorithm. SIMPL modules are both network and programming language agnostic within its supported libraries. However, the story of SIMPL is more about the continuous and pragmatic refinement of our software development toolkit under the open source framework. This book is our attempt to wrap that experience in a package so that others can learn, adopt, and carry on with the journey.

Over the years we have noticed a scarcity of mentoring and apprenticeship in the programming world. Everyone we know has learned pretty much on their own by experimentation or from observing and adopting the style and code of colleagues during a project. The idea of learning directly from a more seasoned person has all but disappeared; there never seems to be time for teaching. The project simply has to get done and out there. Experts are harder to come by because new software tools are coming along with ever increasing frequency. By the time someone has learned enough to be competent, the tool is considered *old* and needs to be *replaced* by the flavour of the month and everyone starts the learning curve again.

In a very real sense, the SIMPL toolbox will never get old and out of date because it is more than a library. SIMPL is also a viewpoint that reinforces modularity and encourages order and structure, all timeless practices for good software developers.

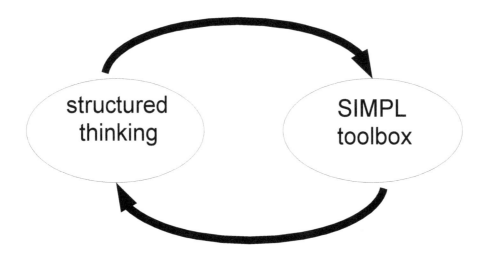

Figure 1: SIMPL Thinking

Who is this book for?

Who is the target audience? A very good question and we wish we had very good answer. Generally speaking, software developers open to new approaches for improving the efficiency and organization of their complex projects will get the most from this book. Advanced programmers should have no difficulty understanding the technical aspects of the book whereas less experienced developers may have to work a little harder. Experience teaches programmers how to recognize patterns and map those from toolkit to project. Experienced SIMPL developers become very adept at discovering software patterns and mapping them into the SIMPL toolkit. However, experienced programmers can become set in their ways. Less entrenched developers will be more open to the SIMPL approaches to software design, structure, testing and project management. While the book discusses various programming languages ('C', Tcl/Tk and Python) and constructs in those languages, it is not a book about programming languages. It is a book about a toolkit and a method for decomposing and handling complex software problems. As such, software project managers and software quality assurance workers could enjoy and learn much from this book. Furthermore, SIMPL is one of many thousands of small open source projects and its story might appeal to others working on similar open source projects.

Useful Background

The SIMPL toolkit and many of the available examples are coded in 'C'. Every effort has been made to keep the 'C' code snips which appear in the book straightforward and heavily commented, but for a full appreciation some knowledge of 'C' is necessary. SIMPL modules are not restricted to the language of the SIMPL library. Tcl/Tk and Python/Tk have been used to illustrate examples in the book as well. Once again, while these code snips are kept straightforward, some background in either or both of these languages will enrich your experience with this material. There is a lot of SIMPL sample code available online including all the code for the project described in the book. For the most complete experience, access to a Linux environment to run these would be helpful. SIMPL was developed for Linux and it is still most at home there.

If you lack any of the above, don't be overly concerned. The story of SIMPL woven into the fabric of this book means that you can still take away many useful ideas.

SIMPL Dilemma

As authors we face a dilemma. How do we illustrate SIMPL in a clear and concise manner when the SIMPL toolkit excels at solving complex problems? If we *dumb down* our example scope we run the risk of leaving the reader with the impression that SIMPL is an overly complex tool to use. Yet, if we illustrate with sufficiently realistic scope we run the risk of losing our point amongst the details of a complex problem.

Our reader must look beyond the simple number of lines of code metric to appreciate the SIMPL examples we use. To fully appreciate the power of SIMPL one must understand its power in the problem decomposition, testing and maintenance phases of a non-trivial project. The *Hello World* type examples are not complex enough to have significant issues with problem decomposition, testing or maintenance. When faced with our illustrative examples we think it helpful to ask some scope expanding *what if* questions such as:

- What if this example were to be run across a network? What if that network consisted of different operating systems on each node?

- What if this was just the first cut in a more complex algorithm? How would the code evolve to an ever more complex feature set? How would you efficiently test this new feature set?

- What if this code required a team of developers to create it in a timely manner? What if that team was geographically dispersed?

There is a sample project contained within the fourth part of the book which faces the SIMPL dilemma. We have attempted to strike a balance between conciseness of explanations and details of scope. Despite this we hope that it will give the reader the essential ideas that lie behind all SIMPL projects: large and small.

Note on Library References

The SIMPL toolkit contains libraries of functions/procedures etc. References to these are made throughout the text and appear as ***emboldened italics*** in order to reinforce their meaning.

Acknowledgements

We would like to take this opportunity to thank all of those people who have worked to make Linux, LaTeX et al. useful and available. Like SIMPL, they are members of the open software movement which we strongly endorse.

We would also like to thank Mohammed El-Korazati, Peter Hiscocks, Graham McCormack, and Peter Spasov for their many valuable and insightful comments on the original manuscript.

Part I

SIMPL Beginnings

Chapter 1

Introduction

1.1   Introduction

To understand what SIMPL (Synchronous Interprocess Messaging Project for Linux) programming is, it is important to step back a bit and ask what software is really all about. Software is what enables hardware to come alive and function in a purposeful way. The art of writing software is similar in many ways to creating anything else, like creating music. Think of hardware as the musical instruments. The software tools such as programming languages, compilers and SIMPL are like musical notes and techniques. You have to learn those first. Having mastered the fundamentals, you can learn to play a few songs that others have written. With lots of practice, you can begin to play those well enough to begin to add your own interpretations. Eventually you get the urge to create entirely new songs of your own. You write a bit, play it back, adjust and eventually arrive at your new musical creation.

Not all software tools allow you to *write a bit, play it back, adjust*. The SIMPL toolset not only allows that approach, it encourages it.

What exactly is SIMPL? SIMPL is really two things. Firstly, SIMPL is an LGPL'd open source library that you can dynamically (or statically) link your code to. Secondly, SIMPL represents a very good paradigm for designing software. It promotes encapsulation of complexity, modularization, testability, and ready extensibility; all good things in a software package.

Much of the software we are familiar with is either so-called shrink wrapped software (eg. Linux distributions or Open Office) or is associated with the Internet (eg. browsers or firewalls). This however, is not where the bulk of software development activity occurs. The largest software markets are associated with the software we rarely see, such as banking systems or embedded software controlling our car engine parameters. Software tools and methodologies evolve as attempts are made to improve the efficiency of the production of this commercial custom software.

Historically, computers themselves were expensive to procure and to operate. In that environment it made sense to apply software methodologies which emphasized as much design and forethought as possible before someone actually sat down to commit it to code and then run it. Large civil engineering projects are like this; you want to do all the design and stress calculations upfront before you start pouring the concrete.

Cracks started to appear in these front-loaded methodologies as computers became less and less expensive per unit of computational power. With modern PCs the cost of running a computer program is vanishingly small. Most of the software development costs are now people costs. With the advent of the Internet and open source tools the cost of entry into software development is now becoming vanishingly small as well. Couple this computer hardware and toolset price point shift with a marketplace which demands increasingly short times to market, and you start to need a radically new software development methodology in order to remain in the game. SIMPL is one such methodology.

A desirable feature of any software toolbox is its ability to encapsulate complexity inherent in many software problems. Object oriented languages use objects to encapsulate functionality. It can be argued that in some cases they also work well to encapsulate complexity. However, in many other cases OOP languages do little to encapsulate the inherent complexity associated with a given software problem. Furthermore, object oriented languages are neither necessarily simple to understand nor to master. One of our aims will be to show that encapsulation of complexity can be done simply.

We will employ the concept of a software IC to illustrate the encapsulation of complexity. Here we will draw on the experience of hardware designers faced with similar complexity issues. It wasn't that many years ago when electronic circuits were built up of discrete components such as transistors, resistors, capacitors, and so on. As complexity of electronic circuits increased it became impossible for hardware engineers to manage this complexity. Enter the integrated circuit (IC). What this did for the hardware engineer was to take functionality which would have previously been provided by a custom circuit board with discrete components and replace it by a silicon chip with well-defined behavioural characteristics and pin outs. This innovation is what has allowed the hardware engineers to make the spectacular progress we have witnessed in the past quarter century.

Software designers never had that equivalent encapsulating technology. Fortunately, modern multitasking operating systems provide us with a ready analogue to the hardware integrated circuit, namely a process running in a protected mode. SIMPL messaging provides the analogue to the IC pins. With SIMPL and a basic language such as 'C' we are going to show that we can achieve something remarkably close to a software IC without having to resort to a complex language or hard to read source code.

Once you have the SIMPL library installed, you can write your modular code such that it readily exchanges Send/Receive/Reply style messages, hence the M-Messaging in the name SIMPL. SIMPL comes with a rich, yet simple set of functions for Interprocess Communication (IPC) (the I-Interprocess in the name). These functions include **name_attach**, **name_locate**, **Send**, **Receive**, **Reply** and a few lesser used and more secondary functions. The SIMPL library API is very lean and clean.

In SIMPL vocabulary we speak of modules (Linux processes) as being one of two types:

- senders

- receivers

Senders compose and send structured messages to receivers. Receivers receive those messages and process them. Until the receiver replies to the sender, the sender is blocked. Until a receiver receives a message, it is blocked. This blocking provides a method of synchronization between processes, hence the S-Synchronous in SIMPL.

SIMPL senders are loosely related to *clients* in the client/server model. The SIMPL receiver is closest to a *server* in that model. In the client/server approach, the primary communication means is usually a TCP/IP socket. Local SIMPL receivers get their messages from a FIFO-synchronized shared memory area. This is not to say that a SIMPL message can't be carried over a TCP/IP socket to a remote SIMPL receiver on another node. In fact, through the use of a surrogate process pair, SIMPL makes such a deployment completely transparent.

SIMPL, the library, treats messages as a raw collection of bytes. We are going to show that if that raw collection is tokenized we can greatly enhance the extensibility of SIMPL modules. This modular encapsulation simplifies things when a number of programmers work in parallel, thus shortening development time. SIMPL teams can also work very independently, often in different geographic locations. Isolating the algorithms into compact modules makes the software easier to debug. Moreover, if a bug is introduced into the software, the affected area will be easier to isolate, retest, and reinstall. We are going to show that the SIMPL Testing Framework (STF) along with the modular SIMPL designs greatly facilitate testability.

1.2   Summary

To summarize the Introduction we can say:

- SIMPL is a software design paradigm promoting encapsulation of complex programs into simpler and more manageable units.

- The SIMPL toolbox contains library functions which allow well-defined message passing between these encapsulated elements.

- SIMPL can be used used locally and/or over a network of host machines.

- SIMPL modules are highly extensible and highly testable.

- SIMPL is a blocked message protocol.

1.3   Next Chapter

In next chapter we will tell the story of SIMPL; how it came about, where it has been used and why it enjoys success.

Chapter 2

A SIMPL Story

2.1 The Story of SIMPL

The journey to SIMPL began in 1988 with a small advertisement from a Canadian company touting a multitasking, real-time OS for PCs of the day. That company was called QNX and the computers of the day were still mostly 286 and 386 machines. The advertisement said that if you called the toll free number they would ship you a self-booting floppy which showed QNX running the Tower of Hanoi game.

We (the authors) were working together at a small battery research company at the time. Our lab was automated with a second hand PDP-11 running Fortran and Assembly Language code. We were looking for a way to introduce PCs into the mix. QNX was successful beyond our wildest expectations. Not only did our 386 computer network (of two) manage the data acquisition and storage requirements for the two thousand battery test stations, it also served that data out to a network of Macintosh workstations. While doing all of this our little network also served as our code development platform.

At the apex we prided ourselves in being able to sit in a technical meeting of battery researchers in the morning and have a fully implemented and tested new software module operational by the end of the same day. What was the key to that ultrafast software design cycle? It was QNX's Send/Receive/Reply messaging scheme. Send/Receive/Reply allowed us to break software problems up into discrete and manageable modules. These modules could then be independently unit tested and finally deployed across our network. QNX was amazing technology considering we were talking about the late 1980s.[1]

---

[1]SIMPL takes the power of Send/Receive/Reply to the Linux operating system.

The SIMPL story resumes about ten years later. In the meantime, we had left the battery research company and started a software development company of our own. One of us (RF) became involved with an AIX project. This project used a middleware product (NetX) to provide an impressive messaging API. Despite the capabilities of this middleware we missed the simplicity of the QNX Send/Receive/Reply API. When the opportunity arose on the AIX project, a Send/Receive/Reply library was created using TCP/IP sockets for message transport. It was clunky and slow but it was only used to create test stubs. This effort was the seed which eventually grew into SIMPL.

A few years later, while between contracts on the AIX effort, we began thinking about a Linux implementation of Send/Receive/Reply. Why Linux? Having used QNX on many projects during that last ten years, we began to experience difficulties in dealing with the company from a business standpoint because QNX began to put increasing emphasis on large multiple license accounts. Furthermore, QNX licensing policies were not as open as some of our customers wanted. From a technical standpoint QNX was still the best OS we had ever used but getting timely device drivers for newer off-the-shelf hardware was increasingly a problem. Moreover, QNX was not always willing to provide the necessary compatibility information to write our own drivers. We needed to break free of this situation but didn't want to lose the QNX tools we came to know and rely on. Around the same time, Linux was beginning to hit its stride.

While the TCP/IP based implementation for AIX formed the starting point it was quickly rejected as being too complex. We decided to try to develop the Send/Receive/Reply messaging scheme from two very different directions, namely: a) SIMPL and b) SIPC. SIMPL is based on a user space FIFO-synchronized shared memory scheme which remains at the core of the SIMPL library today. SIPC (Synchronous InterProcess Communications) was based on a kernel module approach. RF worked on the initial SIMPL and JC worked on the SIPC approach. It is worth mentioning that our friends at Cogent Real-Time Systems Inc. also made a functioning SIPC-type of messaging system and to our knowledge it is still operating today.

SIPC was initially very successful. It was perhaps half as fast as the QNX Send/Receive/Reply benchmark which we considered to be beyond expectations. Being largely kernel-based it was less subject to context switching slow downs resulting in decent performance. It was a treat to be able to write kernel modules without bureaucratic interference and the first version of the SIPC module was written for Linux version 2.0.36. As Linux itself progressed the issues of maintaining the SIPC kernel became obvious. With progressive major version releases the file operations structure was constantly changed. This meant that the SIPC module had to be changed to mirror each new Linux version. This is not a big issue and judicious use of a make-file can handle much of this. But added to this is the fact that we had to support two separate libraries: the SIPC system call library and the user space program library as well, and this starts to become more complicated. Moreover, kernel-based programming is not the usual garden variety application programming for reasons beyond the scope of this book. Other issues arguing against a kernel-based approach were questions of portability to other operating systems which support ANSI 'C' tools. Suffice to say that this was planned to be an open source project and we wanted future development to be unencumbered. Consequently, despite its faster messaging, we abandoned SIPC for the slower but much more general user-space approach of SIMPL. Given the local processing speeds of today's CPUs one has to ask just how fast is fast anyway? As well, given that much of SIMPL's applicability is network-based, network transmission speed slow downs more than overshadow local processing differences.

Around the time that the earliest SIMPL library was taking shape (1999), we were approached to do an embedded acquisition and control project. That project was originally spec'd for QNX but eventually landed on Linux. Thus the first user for the nascent SIMPL library was born. This early implementation of SIMPL proved to be surprisingly robust. This was probably due to the underlying simplicity of a user space FIFO plus shared memory implementation. Despite this simplistic approach SIMPL was benchmarking within an order of magnitude of QNX on the same hardware. It was during this early period (1999-2000) that SIMPL gained its first network surrogates. Those network surrogates made transparent TCP/IP transport of SIMPL messages possible.

The first of these surrogates is still known by its original name: tclSurrogate. It was thus named because its original intent was to allow Tcl/Tk applets to behave as well-formed SIMPL modules in a Linux network. The tclSurrogate and its accompanying protocol are still used to connect Tcl/Tk SIMPL applications across disparate OSs. Its uses are not restricted to that narrow niche. This protocol has been embedded in at least one deeply embedded network appliance (IO Anywhere). This same protocol has been used to allow a Visual Basic application to act as a SIMPL module.

The tclSurrogate was never a true surrogate in the QNX sense. To achieve true QNX style network transparency a new surrogate protocol and architecture was required. We also needed a simple mechanism to extend our SIMPL naming scheme to other network nodes. While QNX supported a network wide name propagation, we chose to extend the SIMPL name into a kind of SIMPL URL. Armed with this design the earliest implementation of the TCP/IP surrogates

(2000) gave SIMPL its first claim to network transparency.

Everything worked and was quite robust. However, as SIMPL came to be deployed in more extensive applications it became clear that the original API wasn't as clean as it could have been. A memory mapped file implementation for the SIMPL sandbox was particularly stressed when SIMPL applications began to contain rapidly spawned processes.

As SIMPL 2.0 took shape (2001-2002), the API was cleaned up considerably and with some redesign the memory mapped file table was completely eliminated. This enhanced the robustness of SIMPL enough to merit the major version increment, but it also meant that SIMPL users faced their first major API change. SIMPL supported both APIs for a transition period. However, once developers recognized that the newer API was both simpler and superior, the old API was gradually deprecated and eventually dropped entirely.

SIMPL was extended to operate with MAC OS X. With this addition networks became more heterogeneous and the endian issue became relevant. Accordingly, the SIMPL network communications underlying remote message exchange which had always been binary in nature were then augmented to be either binary-based or character-based. The SIMPL library was originally only static but the ability to dynamically link was also added.

By 2003 a Python SIMPL library had been added. In this way, Python programs can send and receive messages to each other or to 'C' programs or anything else that is capable of SIMPL communications for that matter. Python has some very appealing programming properties; just ask any Python enthusiast!

By 2004 SIMPL had been deployed in numerous networked configurations. The original TCP/IP surrogate implementation was still reasonably robust but was beginning to show its warts. A redesign and simplification was in order. This TCP/IP surrogate simplification and redesign effort culminated in the SIMPL 3.0 release. A pleasant consequence of this simplification effort turned out to be a marked improvement in SIMPL 3.0's ability to clean up and recover from unplanned network failures. The core SIMPL API didn't change much for SIMPL 3.0 so the migration issues for existing users were minor.

As we write this, SIMPL is a relatively stable project. It has a Sourceforge presence which consistently ranks in the top 20% of its class. It has been downloaded by thousands of users. We don't always get informed where SIMPL is being used. We know it has been used for security systems, banking system test cradles, data acquisition in teaching labs, automated packaging lines, and ports of QNX code to Linux.

Contributions to the SIMPL project still occur from time to time. Recently a new surrogate for RS-232 has been added as a new protocol. Such contributions have allowed SIMPL modules to be written in 'C', C++, Tcl/Tk, Python and JAVA. One of us (RF) runs a no-fee online Linux programming tutorial.[2] Several thousand students have been exposed to the SIMPL way of programming through that course.

2.2 SIMPL Stories

In 1998 John Ousterhaut[3] wrote a paper on the evolution of languages used to create software programs. The paper discussed the differences between scripting languages (like Tcl) and system languages (like 'C' and C++). His thesis was that system languages were designed to efficiently handle complex data structures and algorithms while scripting languages were designed for gluing already working algorithms together. Scripting languages are typically interpreted rather than compiled, so they trade off raw execution speed for better time to market and code resiliency. In other words, scripting languages offer *good enough* performance and get a working application up and running more quickly than compiled languages do. In addition scripted applications are more readily changed as requirements for new feature sets come forward.

The SIMPL toolkit also excels at gluing. Modular SIMPL applications also represent a tradoff of raw execution speed for better time to market and application resiliency when compared against monolithic application architectures.

SIMPL is not the appropriate tool to build a high performance finite element algorithm, but you could use SIMPL to build interfacing modules (such as a GUI) to such an engine.

Low latency real time systems are not the domain of SIMPL, but SIMPL has been coupled with various Linux real time patches (eg. RTLinux) to form a moderate latency real time application. For an even higher performing real time system the Send/Receive/Reply architecture of SIMPL is modelled after one of the premier real time operating systems called QNX.

There are special tools for developing high transaction volume multithreaded applications, but for more moderate data acquisition applications SIMPL is ideally suited. SIMPL has been used to build a testing cradle for one such high transaction banking system. In that instance the flexibility and deterministic nature of the Send/Receive/Reply allowed that cradle to be built and deployed

---

[2]The iCanProgram online courses are available at:
http://www.icanprogram.com/nofeecourses.html.

[3]Scripting: Higher Level Programming for the 21st Century http://home.pacbell.net/ouster/scripting.html

in a matter of weeks. SIMPL has been used in many low transaction rate (less than 100 samples per second) data acquisition applications. In one such application SIMPL was used to create a polling hardware handler, datastore, replicator, configurator, and applet based GUI using 'C', Tcl/Tk, and RTLinux from spec to deployment in less than six weeks.

Deeply embedded appliances typically require highly efficient code. Linux and SIMPL are too high level for these applications. However, SIMPL has been used to glue one such appliance to a broader SIMPL application. As proof of SIMPL's resilience a demo of a SIMPL enabled embedded appliance was assembled offsite in one week, unit tested without access to the larger SIMPL application to which it was to interface and deployed against that larger application without any changes in less than one hour.

SIMPL doesn't often get used to re-architect or port many legacy applications, but SIMPL has been used to extend the reach of such applications. In one instance SIMPL was used to join a laboratory data acquisition system to a legacy UNIX based graphing package. In fact SIMPL has even been used to extend the reach of legacy QNX applications which would otherwise be too expensive to port.

You could use SIMPL for single programmer projects, but the SIMPL toolkit really excels in complex projects which require a multidisciplinary/multilanguage team of developers. In one such project, a team of four programmers was able to build a SIMPL application consisting of a touch screen man/machine interface, PLC interface, printer managers, mainframe XML host interfaces and state machine logic engine in four weeks from beginning to factory floor deployment. The ability to modularize the application and then develop and test each SIMPL module in isolation was key to the success that project. The fact that different modules could be created in different languages (Tcl/Tk, 'C' and Python) was also key to the time to market.

You would not use SIMPL to build a dynamic website, but SIMPL has been used to build several Internet distributed applications (eg.building/home automation). Many other SIMPL applications have been distributed across multiple nodes in a local TCP/IP network. Through the use of surrogates the SIMPL developers need not concern themselves with any of the details associated with transporting messages across networks. SIMPL modules are developed locally and then deployed network wide, often without even a recompile.

Most SIMPL applications are built under Linux. Linux is the OS that SIMPL was designed for. However, the SIMPL library has been ported to other UNIX-like operating systems (eg. AIX and MAC OS X) and reports are that it works well there. Many SIMPL applications are hybrids between multiple operating systems. (eg. Windows and Linux). While in those cases the Windows system is *tricked* into thinking that it knows how to run SIMPL, neither the developer nor the user need to concern themselves with those details. The illusion is seamless.

Not all SIMPL projects succeed. SIMPL promotes a problem decomposition strategy which, if done well, will amplify the chances of success. However, if done poorly it can achieve the opposite. Furthermore, not all project management structures are in tune with resilient architectures that can be added to and changed with ease. Many front loaded, top down design paradigms assume that all has to be known about a problem before coding can begin. Change control is often a cumbersome and bureaucratic process designed in part to *discourage* changes to the application. These structures are poorly adapted to take advantage of the power of SIMPL. It is no fluke that SIMPL is an open source project. The open source design paradigm is ideally suited to the SIMPL way.

2.3   Summary

The story of SIMPL can be summarized as follows:

- SIMPL takes its form based on the message passing paradigm used by the QNX operating system in the 1980s.

- SIMPL takes this operational structure from the QNX platform to other platforms, most notably Linux.

- SIMPL uses a surrogate approach to broaden its scope from message passing communications between processes local to one host to message passing between processes on different host machines.

- SIMPL libraries exist so far for 'C', Python and Tcl.

- SIMPL surrogates exist for the TCP/IP and RS-232 protocols.

2.4   Next Chapter

In the next chapter we are going to discuss the concept of softwareICs and how they are to software designs what traditional electronic ICs are to PC board layouts.

Part II

SIMPL Elements

Chapter 3

SoftwareICs: Theory

"Complexity must be grown from simple systems that already work." –Kevin Kelly [1]

3.1 SoftwareICs

Computer hardware is complex, so is computer software. In fact as the cost per unit of computational horsepower continues to decrease, user demands on software applications have become ever more complex. Unfortunately, with all this increased software complexity comes problems associated with creating robust software in a cost effective and timely manner.

A number of years ago hardware engineers faced similar issues. Before the advent of Integrated Circuits (ICs), electronic circuits were built up of discrete components (transistors, resistors, capacitors etc.) all interconnected with printed circuit boards and wires. As complexity of electronic circuits increased it became increasingly difficult for hardware engineers to manage this intricacy. This difficulty adversely affected the scope and cost of products as well as their time to market.

With the advent of ICs much of this complexity began to be hidden inside the chips themselves. Thousands of discrete components were replaced by a silicon chip with well-defined functionality and pinouts. The inner workings of the chips themselves where incredibly complex, but the integration of the chip

---

[1]Out of Control: The New Biology of Machines, Social Systems, and the Economic World by Kevin Kelly, Addison-Wesley Pub., 1994, ISBN 0-210-48340-8

into any given design was much more manageable. The job of designing complex functionality into products became much easier.

Complexity was encapsulated and miniaturized. This complexity encapsulating innovation is what has allowed hardware engineers to make such spectacular progress. The concept of a hardware design as an interconnected series of islands of complexity represented a huge architectural shift. The advent of ICs allowed the hardware designer to use a given chip in a product design without having to understand circuits within the chip itself. As long as the designer conformed to the specifications of the external interface to the chip (pins), the chip would react in a very predictable manner.

This is what encapsulation of complexity offers:

- Complexity hiding.

- Predictable/reproducible behavior.

Software is still created out of discrete components and painstakingly hand-coded to form an application. Software has hit a scope and complexity wall similar to that faced by the pre-IC hardware world. Custom software projects often go over budget and underdeliver on ever more complex user requirements.

Software engineers should look to their hardware counterparts for better approaches to managing complexity. What software needs is that equivalent encapsulating technology to the IC: what we are going to call the *softwareIC*.

Object Oriented Programming (OOP) languages such as C++ or JAVA attempt to attack the software complexity problem at the programming language level. For some classes of problems such as GUI and database design they have been successful. For whole other classes of problems OOP languages have only succeeded in shifting complexity to other areas in the software development chain such as testing, toolsets, class library design, maintenance or the learning curve. At best objects in software design offer partial complexity hiding. The software designer still has to know and master a complex language (e.g., C++) in order to be able to wire objects together into a product. Often the toolkit itself dictates which language is used for all aspects of a particular application.

In our opinion, true encapsulation of complexity behind a universally simple and extendable API is required to produce a softwareIC. The software designer should not have to master a complex object-oriented language and toolset in order to be able to *wire together* these softwareICs. At the very least the software designer should be able to choose the wiring language independent of the chip language.

With the advent of wide area networks such as the Internet, software applications are increasingly distributed and multiprocessed. In such situations the choice of a message passing paradigm often unintentionally introduces a degree of unpredictability and randomness into a software product. It has been said that client/server software design does not handle complexity well. If the client and the server are not regularly brought into synchronization it is exceedingly difficult to replicate or predict all possible states of a multiprocessing system. Much depends on the environment and timing of these processes. Modules may work fine in one environment and suffer sporadic failures in another. This leads to increased code complexity as well as increased testing and maintenance costs, all resulting in a poorer quality software product. Often the blame is incorrectly directed at the multiprocess design paradigm. We agree with the original designers of Send/Receive/Reply synchronized messaging who believed that the answer lies in forcing a state-machine-like synchronization to occur on each message pass.

Many have argued that this blocking/forced synchronization introduces unnecessary complexity into a message exchange, but when properly applied it achieves exactly the opposite effect. By forcing synchronization to occur at each message pass, one finds that multiprocess applications behave in a very predictable and reproducible manner. Gone are the timing and environmental effects that plague nonsynchronized message passing schemes. After all, one of the oldest blocking/forced synchronized message passing schemes is the simple function call using the stack for message transport. When dealing with complex applications, predictability and reproducibility of behavior represent a great strategic advantage.

With Send/Receive/Reply systems, the sender is blocked during message transmission and explicitly unblocked by the receiver process with the reply. As such it is very easy to arrange to transport these messages over a variety of media (including some which are *slow*). The messages could be exchanged via shared memory if the processes were on the same processor, or via the Internet if the processes were physically separated or on a serial line in a dial up or radio modem situation. While the throughput of the collective of processes would be affected by the message transmission speed, the performance would be predictable and reproducible.

Software *must* be predictable for reliable testing. Nothing makes software QA people wish for a career change more than an application which exhibits unpredictable and unreproducible behavior. Predictability and reproducibility of behavior is an essential requirement for a softwareIC.

Fortunately, modern multitasking operating systems provide us with a ready

analogue to the hardware integrated circuit: a user space process running in a
protected mode. If one of those processes encounters a fatal error it rarely brings
down the whole machine even if something sends a process into a locked state.

Many real time operating systems (RTOSs) have pioneered the use of user-
space processes as an encapsulation scheme. One of the oldest to use this scheme
is QNX. Since 1980, QNX has released a continuous series of innovative operating systems that were based upon a set of cooperating processes using a
Send/Receive/Reply messaging paradigm. QNX's approach to kernel design differs greatly from that used in Linux and we do not wish to reinflame the infamous
microkernel vs. monolithic kernel debate. Suffice to say that we believe that the
process model and the Send/Receive/Reply messaging paradigm first pioneered
by QNX offers the key ingredients of a successful softwareIC.

Fortunately in the SIMPL toolkit, with its QNX heritage, we have an ideal
candidate for the creation of a softwareIC on Linux systems. The Linux user
space process is our chip, the SIMPL Send/Receive/Reply messaging is our
pinout and the message bytes themselves are the interconnecting wires.

3.2   SIMPL Axioms

When development of the SIMPL library and utilities began, the concept of a
softwareIC had yet to be articulated. Nonetheless from its inception, the development of the SIMPL toolkit and its subsequent applicability to the softwareIC
concept has been guided by a set of principles. These principles influenced and
arbitrated all our major design decisions with SIMPL.[2]

The SIMPL axioms are:

Anonymity Neither a SIMPL sender (initiator of messages) nor a SIMPL re-
    ceiver (consumer of messages) can readily discover the name of their SIMPL
    communications partner. This anonymity forms the basis of the ready
    testability of SIMPL modules using stubs as partners.

Need to know A SIMPL sender doesn't need to know where its communication
    partner is (locally or on a network). A SIMPL sender shouldn't need to
    know the details of a communications partner's algorithm. It should only
    need to know the message API. Response timing is the responsibility of the
    SIMPL receiver and not the SIMPL sender. For example, a SIMPL sender

---

[2]Webster's Dictionary defines axiom as: *an established rule or principle or a self-evident
truth.*

should not need to know if a SIMPL receiver is going to hold back a reply or not (a concept known as reply blocking). A SIMPL communicating pair would have to agree on such things as byte ordering and message structures, but to the SIMPL transport layer these are just a collection of bytes. Furthermore, the SIMPL layer should never have to peek into this message structure for any reason.

Democracy SIMPL message exchange sequencing between primitive pairings is always on a first in first out basis. However, with appropriately constructed SIMPL softwareICs you can achieve priority store and forward messaging algorithms. That feature is just not part of the basic SIMPL message transport.

Compile Once, Deploy Anywhere A SIMPL module should not need to code anything with respect to the message transport. A SIMPL module should be able to be compiled, tested locally and then deployed across the network without any recompile.

KISS Whenever we were faced with decisions with multiple paths we always endeavoured to choose the simplest path which had any useful value and implement that. The SIMPL API is deliberately basic. The choice to use a colon delimited composite SIMPL name to allow network transparency is also deliberately basic.

Timeouts Over the years many users have asked for SIMPL *Send* timeouts. We've come to believe that no application should need this feature. Whenever we've arrived at a design where we thought we needed such a timeout there was always a better way of looking at the layout which negated that need. There are timeouts internal to SIMPL surrogates which endeavour to add robustness to the message transport algorithm. When these timeouts kick in they always appear to the SIMPL modules as *Send* or *Reply* failures.

Security We believe that SIMPL applications themselves should look after any security aspects required. In other words, if encrypted messages and certificates are required they belong at the SIMPL application layer and not as part of SIMPL itself.

3.3   SIMPL as a SoftwareIC Toolkit

The softwareIC as a concept is more general than SIMPL. SoftwareICs could be written with toolkits other than SIMPL. We have found that SIMPL is a great toolkit for creating general purpose softwareICs on a Linux platform. Here are some of the reasons why.

The SIMPL library, and many of the projects which use SIMPL have been written in 'C'. However, hooks to allow the creation of SIMPL modules in Python, Tcl/Tk and C++ have been made available as the SIMPL toolkit has matured. This means that a SIMPL softwareIC can be written in the most appropriate language for its algorithm rather than the language dictated by the choice of an OOP toolkit. SIMPL modules created in these different languages can be mixed in a given SIMPL application. The language used to write the SIMPL softwareIC itself in no way dictates the language of another SIMPL module with which interaction takes place. Furthermore, a given SIMPL process has no way of discovering which language was used to construct another softwareIC with which it is exchanging a message.

A properly constructed SIMPL softwareIC has no need to know or discover the physical location of its exchange partners. This means that the same binary image can be tested with local message exchanges and then deployed with remote message exchanges (see chapter 7). Overall collective application performance would differ but the individual softwareIC would not need to change in any way. In may instances even a recompile is unnecessary.

A SIMPL softwareIC is completely insulated from the internal algorithm of an exchange partner. This means that test stubs can be created which completely simulate and replicate the environment surrounding a softwareIC. In particular, error conditions which would be costly or difficult to reproduce in the full system can be simulated in a test environment. This means that SIMPL softwareICs can be rigorously tested before being deployed (or redeployed) in the real world application.

SIMPL softwareICs lend themselves well to projects with multiple developers. SIMPL applications of any complexity contain multiple SIMPL modules. Once the messaging API is agreed upon, work can procede in parallel with each SIMPL module in a given application. The implementation details of a SIMPL enabled process cannot affect any interacting process provided that implementation conforms to the agreed upon message API. While a poor softwareIC implementation will affect the overall application performance adversely, the application will still operate. Once a poor algorithm has been identified it can optimized in isolation from the rest of the application. Once fully tested, this reworked softwareIC can be inserted into the application without even recompiling the adjacent software-ICs.

When faced with designing an application using the SIMPL toolkit, it used to be that one would sketch out a *circuit board* with the basic SIMPL primitives: senders and receivers. This works for basic projects, but over the years the SIMPL project has accumulated an extensive codebase of useful frameworks and example code which we have called our softwareICs repository. Now when SIMPL designers begin designing complex applications, they can sketch out *circuit boards* with senders, receivers, proxies, broadcasters, agencies, relays etc. SIMPL softwareICs have one thing which distinguishes themselves from their hardware cousins: they are inherently extendable and adaptable.

3.4   Summary

In summary here is why SIMPL softwareICs represent a better way to design complex software applications:

- In principle SIMPL softwareICs can be written in any language.

- The language used to write the softwareIC itself in no way dictates the language of another softwareIC with which interaction takes place.

- A properly constructed SIMPL softwareIC has no need to know or discover the physical location of its exchange partner.

- A SIMPL softwareIC is completely insulated from the internal algorithm of an exchange partner.

- SIMPL softwareICs lend themselves well to complex projects with multiple developers.

- The public SIMPL softwareICs repository represents an increasingly useful body of seed code for any given project.

As was the case with the advent of hardware ICs, this softwareIC approach to software development lowers project risk/cost and allows ever more complex applications to be brought to market in a timely manner.

3.5 Next Chapter

In the next chapter we will study the details of the core library functions of
SIMPL. We are going to look at how local SIMPL communications are added
into program code and how processes pass messages.

Chapter 4

SIMPL Core

Previously we introduced you to the SIMPL design paradigm. We also gave you a flavour for the motivation in creating SIMPL with a short description of its history. In this chapter we are going to dive a little deeper into the core SIMPL library.

Before beginning that discourse, allow us to use an analogy. Two co-operating SIMPL processes are like two individuals about to engage in a phone conversation. The conversation initiator (SIMPL sender) would need to know the phone number (receiver ID) of the other party (SIMPL receiver). Normally this conversation initiator would know some identifying information about the intended conversation partner: likely the person's name (SIMPL name). To obtain the phone number (receiver ID) a look up by name (*name_locate*) in either an address book (FIFO_PATH) or a phone book would be required. To be able to cross-reference the person's name with a phone number meant that that person would have previously supplied information to the indexing organization (*name_attach*). Armed with the phone number, the phone conversation can be initiated by dialing (**Send**). When the intended conversation partner picks up the call (**Receive**) a conversation can ensue. At this point our analogy breaks down somewhat because a SIMPL conversation is more like a two way radio conversation than a phone conversation. In a two way radio call only one person can speak at a time and the conversation takes on a talk-response-talk-response (Send - Reply - Send - Reply) characteristic.

In the following section we will be referring back to this telephone analogy as we discuss SIMPL communications restricted to processes running on one host computer.

Telephone	SIMPL
telephone client name	SIMPL name
telephone listing	name_attach
telephone number	SIMPL ID
telephone number lookup	name_locate

Table 4.1: Telephone/SIMPL Analogy

4.1   Local SIMPL

The purpose of this section is to discuss the inner workings of SIMPL on a *local* level. By *local* we are referring to the method of operation used by SIMPL to enable communications between processes running on a single host computer. Core SIMPL is only functional at a local level. In order to extend this core functionality across a network, we rely on the notion of surrogates. We will be discussing surrogates at length later on in the book.[1]

4.1.1   SIMPL Names

ALL processes that use SIMPL *must* be uniquely named per host computer. In our telephone analogy this is equivalent to saying that there can only be one *John_Smith* listed for any given city. The SIMPL library will enforce this rule, so it is up to the SIMPL programmer to ensure a set of unique SIMPL names for the modules running on any given node. For what follows let's call this unique name the "SIMPL name". It is a string of characters and is the analogue to the name of the person we are trying to call. A SIMPL process names itself by making the **name_attach**("SIMPL name") library call. This is normally the first order of business in any SIMPL program. Once a SIMPL module is named it can engage in SIMPL communications.

To initiate this communication a SIMPL sender process will make the **name_locate**("SIMPL name") function call to return a unique integer called the SIMPL ID. In our telephone analogy the SIMPL ID is the telephone number and the **name_locate** call is the act of looking the number up. Once a sender process has obtained the unique SIMPL ID of a receiver process, it is then able to initiate a message exchange via the **Send** library call. .

The above can be summed up in the table below:

---
[1]For detailed information on surrogate processes see Chapter 7.

4.1.2   SIMPL Messaging

In a local SIMPL message exchange, the message data is written by the sender into an area of shared memory owned by the sender. This memory is *shared* because the receiver will also be reading from it. This shared memory is identified on the host system by a unique integer called the shared memory ID. The *transport* of this message data from the sender to the receiver is coordinated by the exchange of this shared memory ID over a FIFO owned by the receiver. See Figure 4.1.

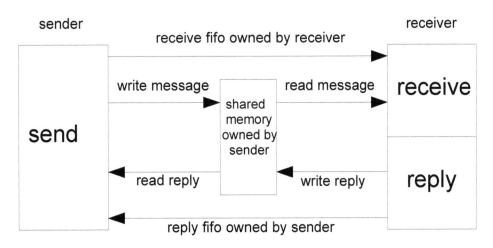

Figure 4.1: Send/Receive/Reply (SRY)

The receiver is read-blocked while it awaits the arrival of a shared memory ID on its FIFO. In effect, this receiver process does nothing until it reads a shared memory ID written to the FIFO by a sender. When such a shared memory ID arrives the receiver is unblocked from reading the FIFO, copies the message from the sender's shared memory, processes the message in some pre-ordained way and then replies back to the sender. Once the sender has read this reply the receiver usually goes back to trying to read its receive FIFO. ie. goes back into a blocked state. In this way we have a natural queuing and serialization of the message flow into the SIMPL receiver. All we need to do now is to arrange to have the sender block on its reply FIFO after posting a message and we have achieved full synchronization of message and response. Furthermore, the receiver can utilize the same shared memory area owned by the sender to post its response with full confidence that the sender will not be modifying that area in its reply-blocked state. The sender will remain reply-blocked until the receiver has completed the transfer. Recall that *blocking* in this case means that the process will cease to run until it is explicitly unblocked by the initiator of the message. Receive-blocked receivers get unblocked by a **Send** from a sender. Reply-blocked senders get unblocked by the **Reply** from a receiver. In SIMPL terminology we call this mechanism Send/Receive/Reply or SRY for short.

Keeping Figure 4.1 in mind, let's look at what happens during a typical message exchange.

1. The receiver is receive-blocked. That is, it awaits an integer message via its receive FIFO.

2. The sender loads its shared memory with the contents of a data message.

3. The sender writes its shared memory ID to the FIFO via the integer message.

4. The sender now becomes reply-blocked and awaits a response from the receiver on the reply FIFO.

5. The receiver reads the integer message from the FIFO. The value of the integer tells the receiver what shared memory to open.

6. The receiver opens the shared memory, reads the message header and the appropriate contents.

7. The receiver processes the message and forms a reply for the sender.

8. The receiver replies back to the sender by loading the sender's shared memory with the reply data message and then writes an integer message on the reply FIFO.

9. The sender reads the integer message on the reply FIFO, becomes unblocked and then reads the reply data message from the shared memory and processes it.

There are three important items to emphasize. Firstly, the shared memory is owned by the sender, not the receiver. The main reason for this is that if it were owned by the receiver, and there was more than one sender, then messages could be overwritten. This shared memory is allocated when the sender sends its first message and is deallocated if the sender terminates. Secondly, the reading and writing of the FIFOs is atomic, as evidenced by the integer message referred to above. Making the FIFO *message* atomic ensures that any messages written to and read from the FIFOs are performed with a minimum of overhead. This is the mechanism that SIMPL uses to synchronize the sending and receiving of data messages. Thirdly, the receive FIFO is owned by the receiver but the reply FIFO is owned by the sender. In this way, messages to a receiver get naturally queued but any given sender only receives one reply FIFO message at a time.

In order for a program to use SIMPL, the shared memory and FIFOs must already be configured within the program. This configuring is the task of the *name_attach* call. All programs which desire to utilize SIMPL must make this call prior to any other SIMPL function calls such as *Send*, *Receive*, *Reply*. The purpose of this call is to set up the necessary elements for all local SIMPL communications. The important part of this functionality is that the two FIFOs are made in the FIFO_PATH directory (see Chapter 9): the first is called the receive FIFO and the second is called the reply FIFO. The actual names of the FIFOs are a combination of the SIMPL name and the PID (process identification) of the calling program; hence the FIFO names are themselves unique to the computer. This uniqueness is of paramount importance as this provides the SIMPL *addressing* scheme for getting messages to and from the correct processes.

If you recall in our analogy above, the *name_attach* call is analogous to registering your name with the phone company so that it will appear in the phone book. The analogue to looking up the phone number in that phone book is the *name_locate* call. You couldn't look someone up in the phone book until that person had registered their information with the phone book publisher. Therefore in a SIMPL system it is imperative that the relevant processes are started in the correct order. Since a SIMPL sender must perform a *name_locate* call to open the prospective receiver's receive FIFO for writing, that SIMPL receiver must have already performed a *name_attach* to create this FIFO. The *name_locate* call returns a file descriptor to the receiver's receive FIFO.

At this point we should recap. Let's do this by looking at how a receiver and a sender would set up and use SIMPL.

Receiver Steps

R1. The receiver allocates adequate memory for incoming and outgoing messages - only required for 'C' programs *usually*.

R2. The receiver performs a *name_attach* call. This enables all of the necessary mechanisms required to use SIMPL on the receiver's side.

R3. The receiver makes a *Receive* call and becomes receive-blocked awaiting any incoming messages from senders.

R4. Upon receiving a message, the receiver presumably processes the message and forms a reply message.

R5. The receiver makes a **Reply** call and returns the reply message to the sender.

R6. When the program is finished, the **name_detach** call releases all SIMPL components. This call is present for completeness and is a good idea to include in the program but it should be understood that under a normal program termination any SIMPL components will be released by default.

Sender Steps

S1. The sender allocates adequate memory for incoming and outgoing messages - only required for 'C' programs *usually*.

S2. The sender performs a **name_attach** call. This enables all of the necessary mechanisms required to use SIMPL on the sender's side.

S3. The sender performs a **name_locate** call to open a channel to the intended receiver.

S4. The sender composes the message to be sent.

S5. The sender makes a **Send** call to the receiver and becomes reply-blocked awaiting the reply message from the receiver.

S6. Upon obtaining a reply, the sender carries on with its programming and presumably using the contents of the replied message.

S7. See R6 above.

4.2   SRY Example

In the following example we are going to illustrate how a sender program and a receiver program use SIMPL in order to communicate with one and other. The sender will send ten messages to the receiver consisting of an integer valued from 1 to 10, one at a time. The receiver will square the integer and reply the result to the sender who will print out the original number and the squared number. This example is not meant to be a realistic SIMPL problem but merely to demonstrate how SIMPL communications work from a code standpoint.

Note that both the receiver and the sender programs are written in 'C', Tcl, and Python and are arranged in no particular order. This is because *any* sender can send the message to *any* receiver. The Tcl sender program can send the message to the 'C' receiver program if desired or the Python sender can send the message to the Tcl receiver or the 'C' sender can send the message to the 'C' receiver and so on. Feel free to choose the sender/receiver code snips written in the language you are most comfortable with because they all do the same things and carry the same commentary.[2]

In each code snip the *Receiver Steps* R1-R5 and the *Sender Steps* S1-S5 listed earlier are indicated as comments on the appropriate lines when applicable.

4.2.1 The Receivers

The Tcl Receiver

```
1   # Tcl receiver: program called tcl_receiver.tcl
2
3   #!/usr/bin/tclsh
4
5   # initialize variables
6   set myName receiver
7   lappend auto_path $env(SIMPL_HOME)/lib
8   package require Fctclx
9
10  # perform simpl name attach
11  set myslot [name_attach $myName]                              ;# R2
12  if { [string compare $myslot "NULL"] == 0 } {
13      puts stdout [format "%s: cannot attach name" $myName]
14      exit
15      }
16
17  while { 1 } {
18      # receive incoming messages
19      set buf [Receive]                                         ;# R3
20      binary scan $buf i1i1 fromWhom nbytes
21      if {$nbytes == -1} {
22          puts stdout [format "%s: receive error" $myName]
23          continue
24          }
```

_____

[2]If you want to follow along without transcribing these examples the source is available online at http://www.icanprogram.com/simplBook

```
25    binary scan $buf x8i1 inNumber
26
27    # calculate square of sent number
28    set outNumber [expr $inNumber * $inNumber]              ;# R4
29
30    # reply squared number to sender
31    set rMsg [binary format "i1" $outNumber]
32    set rBytes [string length $rMsg]
33    Reply $fromWhom $rMsg $rBytes]                           ;# R5
34    }
35
36  name_detach                                               ;# R6
37  exit
```

line 3 Invoke the Tcl interpreter.

line 6 Set unique SIMPL name.

lines 7-8 Include SIMPL library package.

lines 11-15 The program performs a **name_attach**. Recall that this is required prior to any other SIMPL library calls. The argument in the **name_attach** call is the SIMPL name chosen to be unique on the local host. Again, recall the phone book analogy; this is like adding the receiver's name to the phone book.

lines 17-34 This is an infinite loop allowing messages to be received, processed and replied to continuously. Many receiver type programs have this format.

line 19 This is where the program receives incoming messages and places them one at a time into an input buffer.

line 20 The SIMPL ID of the sender and the size of the message are extracted from the input buffer. The receiver needs to know who to reply back to and how many bytes to read from the buffer to obtain the message.

lines 21-24 The incoming message is checked for problems.

line 25 The incoming message content, an integer, is extracted from the input buffer.

line 26 The integer is squared.

lines 31-32 The outgoing message is composed.

line 33 The outgoing message is replied back to the sender.

line 36 The SIMPL program components are removed.

The Python Receiver

```
1   # Python receiver: program called py_receiver.py
2
3   #! /usr/bin/python
4
5   # import necessary modules
6   import sys
7   import struct
8   from simpl import *
9   from psimpl import *
10
11  # initialize necessary variables
12  me = "receiver"
13
14  # perform simpl name attach
15  retVal = name_attach(me)                                       # R2
16  if retVal == -1:
17    print "%s: name attach error-%s" %(me, whatsMyError())
18    sys.exit(-1)
19
20  while 1:
21    # receive incoming messages
22    messageSize, senderId, inBuffer = Receive()                 # R3
23    if messageSize == -1:
24      print "%s: receive error-%s" %(me, whatsMyError())
25      sys.exit(-1)
26    inNumber = getBinaryValue(inBuffer, 0, SINT, "i")
27
28    # calculate square of sent number
29    outNumber = inNumber * inNumber                             # R4
30
31    # reply squared number to sender
32    outBuffer = struct.pack("i", outNumber)
33    if Reply(senderId, outBuffer) == -1:                       # R5
34      print "%s: Reply error-%s" %(me, whatsMyError())
35
36  name_detach()                                                 # R6
```

line 3 Invoke the Python interpreter.

lines 6-9 Import necessary Python and SIMPL modules.

line 12 Set unique SIMPL name.

lines 15-18 The program performs a **name_attach**. Recall that this is required prior to any other SIMPL library calls. The argument in the
name_attach() call is the SIMPL name chosen to be unique on the local host. Again, recall the phone book analogy; this is like adding the
receiver's name to the phone book.

lines 20-34 This is an infinite loop allowing messages to be received, processed
and replied to continuously. Many receiver type programs have this format.

line 22 This is where the program receives incoming messages. The first tuple
value is the size of the message, the second is the sender's SIMPL ID, and
the third is a string type containing the message.

lines 23-25 The incoming message is checked for problems.

line 29 The integer is squared.

lines 32 The outgoing message is composed.

lines 33-34 The **Reply** call returns the result of the squaring process to the
sender. The first argument represents the sender's SIMPL identification
which was gotten from the earlier **Receive** call, the second argument is
the memory containing the squared value of the original integer.

line 36 The SIMPL program components are removed.

The 'C' Receiver

```
1  // 'C' receiver: program called c_receiver
2
3  #include <stdio.h>
4  #include <stdlib.h>
5  #include <unistd.h>
6  #include <simpl.h>
7
8  int main()
9  {
10 char *sender;
11 int inNumber;
12 int outNumber;
13 int size = sizeof(int);                              // R1
14 char *me = "receiver";
15
```

```
16   // perform simpl name attach
17   if (name_attach(me, NULL) == -1)                              // R2
18     {
19     printf("%s: cannot attach name-%s\n", me, whatsMyError());
20     exit(-1);
21     }
22
23   while (1)
24     {
25     // receive incoming messages
26     if (Receive(&sender, &inNumber, size) == -1)                // R3
27       {
28       printf("%s: Receive error-%s\n", me, whatsMyError());
29       continue;
30       }
31
32     // calculate square of sent number
33     outNumber = inNumber * inNumber;                            // R4
34
35     // reply squared number to sender
36     if (Reply(sender, &outNumber, size) == -1)                  // R5
37       {
38       printf("%s: Reply error-%s\n", me, whatsMyError());
39       continue;
40       }
41     }
42
43   name_detach();                                                // R6
44   return(1);
45   }
```

lines 3-5 Include required 'C' header files.

line 6 Include SIMPL header file.

lines 10-14 Variable declarations. Note the receiver program SIMPL name.

lines 17-21 The program performs a ***name_attach***. Recall that this is required
prior to any other SIMPL library calls. The first argument in the function
call is the SIMPL name chosen to be unique on the local host. The second
argument which in our case is NULL, is a pointer to a user-defined function
that would be run at the program's exit. Again, recall the phone book
analogy; this is like adding the receiver's name to the phone book.

lines 23-41 This is an infinite loop allowing messages to be received, processed and replied to continuously. Many receiver type programs have this format.

lines 26-30 This is where the program receives incoming messages. The first argument of the **Receive** call stores the sender's unique SIMPL identification for later use in the **Reply**. The second argument is a pointer to memory where the incoming integer will be copied. The third argument dictates the maximum size of the incoming message in order to prevent any overrun of memory space.

line 33 The incoming integer is squared.

lines 36-40 The **Reply** call returns the result of the squaring process to the sender. The first argument represents the sender's SIMPL identification which was gotten from the earlier **Receive** call, the second argument is a pointer to the memory contining the squared integer and the third argument is size of the replied message.

line 43 The SIMPL program components are removed.

4.2.2   The Senders

The Python Sender

```
1   # Python sender: program called py_sender.py
2
3   #! /usr/bin/python
4
5   # import necessary modules
6   import sys
7   import struct
8   from simpl import *
9   from psimpl import *
10
11  # initialize necessary variables
12  me = "sender"
13  inBuffer = struct.pack("i", 0)                          # S1
14
15  # perform simpl name attach
16  if name_attach(me) == -1:                               # S2
17      print "%s: name attach error-%s" %(me, whatsMyError())
18      sys.exit(-1)
19
```

```
20  # name locate the receiver program
21  receiver = name_locate("receiver")                              # S3
22  if receiver == -1:
23    print "%s: name locate error-%s" %(me, whatsMyError())
24    sys.exit(-1)
25
26  # build and send message to receiver
27  for outNumber in range(1, 11):
28    outBuffer = struct.pack("i", outNumber)                       # S4
29    if Send(receiver, outBuffer, inBuffer) == -1:                 # S5
30      print "%s: send error-%s" %(me, whatsMyError())
31      sys.exit(-1)
32    inNumber = getBinaryValue(inBuffer, 0, SINT, "i")             # S6
33    # print out the messages
34    print "out number=%d in number=%d" %(outNumber, inNumber)
35
36  name_detach()                                                    # S7
```

line 3 Invoke the Python interpreter.

lines 6-9 Import necessary Python and SIMPL modules.

line 12 Set unique SIMPL name.

lines 16-18 The program performs a **name_attach**. Recall that this is required prior to any other SIMPL library calls. The argument in the **name_attach**() call is the SIMPL name chosen to be unique on the local host. Again, recall the phone book analogy; this is like adding the receiver's name to the phone book.

lines 21-24 The sender needs to name locate the receiver program so the various FIFO and shared memory connections can be made. In our phone book analogy this is the same as looking up the phone number in the phone book.

lines 27-34 A loop of ten iterations is run which sends the numbers 1-10 to the receiver, retrieves a reply from the receiver in the form of the square of the sent number and then prints the sent and replied numbers to stdout.

lines 29-31 The **Send** call is the mechanism for sending out the number to be squared and retrieving the result from the receiver. The first argument represents the receiver's SIMPL ID which was gotten from the earlier **name_locate** call, the second argument is a memory buffer containing the

integer to be sent to the receiver, the third argument is a memory buffer
that will contain the reply from the receiver.

line 36 The SIMPL program components are removed.

The 'C' Sender

```
1   // 'C' sender: program called c_sender
2
3   #include <stdio.h>
4   #include <stdlib.h>
5   #include <unistd.h>
6   #include <simpl.h>
7
8   int main()
9   {
10  int receiver;
11  int inNumber;
12  int outNumber;
13  int size = sizeof(int);                                    // S1
14  char *me = "sender";
15
16  // perform simpl name attach
17  if (name_attach(me, NULL) == -1)                           // S2
18     {
19     printf("%s: cannot attach name-%s\n", me, whatsMyError());
20     exit(-1);
21     }
22
23  // name locate the receiver program
24  receiver = name_locate("receiver");                        // S3
25  if (receiver == -1)
26     {
27     printf("%s: cannot locate receiver-%s\n", me, whatsMyError());
28     exit(-1);
29     }
30
31  // build message and send to receiver
32  for (outNumber = 1; outNumber <= 10; outNumber++)          // S4
33     {
34     if (Send(receiver, &outNumber, &inNumber, size, size) == -1)// S5
35        {
36        printf("%s: cannot send to receiver-%s\n", me, whatsMyError());
37        exit(-1);
38        }
39     // print out the messages
40     printf("out number=%d in number=%d\n", outNumber, inNumber);// S6
```

```
41      }
42
43    name_detach ();                                                          // S7
44    return ( 1 );
45    }
```

lines 3-5 Include required 'C' header files.

line 6 Include SIMPL header file.

lines 10-14 Variable declarations. Note the sender program SIMPL name.

lines 17-21 The program performs a **name_attach**. Recall that this is required
prior to any other SIMPL library calls. The first argument in the function
call is the SIMPL name chosen to be unique on the local host. The second
argument which in our case is NULL, is pointer to a user-defined function
that would be run at the program's exit. Again, recall the phone book
analogy; this is like adding the sender's name to the phone book.

lines 21-24 The sender needs to name locate the receiver program so the various
FIFO and shared memory connections can be made. In our phone book
analogy this is the same as looking up the phone number in the phone
book.

lines 32-41 A loop of ten iterations is run which sends the numbers 1-10 to the
receiver, retrieves a reply from the receiver in the form of the square of the
sent number and then prints the sent and replied numbers to stdout.

lines 34-38 The **Send** call is the mechanism for sending out the number to
be squared and retrieving the result from the receiver. The first argument represents the receiver's SIMPL ID which was gotten from the earlier **name_locate** call, the second argument is a pointer to the memory
containing the number to be sent to the receiver, the third argument is a
pointer to the memory that will contain the reply from the receiver, the
fourth argument is the size in bytes of the second argument and finally, the
fifth argument is the size of the reply message from the receiver in bytes.

line 43 The SIMPL program components are removed.

The Tcl Sender

```
1   # Tcl sender: program tcl_sender.tcl
2
3   #!/usr/bin/tclsh
4
5   # initialize variables
6   set myName sender
7   lappend auto_path $env(SIMPL_HOME)/lib
8   package require Fctclx
9
10  # perform simpl name attach
11  set myslot [name_attach $myName]                                        ;# S2
12  if { [string compare $myslot "NULL"] == 0 } {
13      puts stdout [format "%s: cannot attach name" $myName]
14      exit
15      }
16
17  # name locate the receiver program based on its SIMPL name
18  set recvID [name_locate "receiver"]                                     ;# S3
19  if {$recvID == -1} {
20      puts stdout [format "%s: cannot locate receiver" $myName]
21      name_detach
22      exit
23      }
24
25  # compose and Send message; retrieve reply and display
26  for {set outNumber 1} { $outNumber <= 10} {incr outNumber} {
27      set sMsg [binary format "i1" $outNumber]                            ;# S4
28      set sBytes [string length $sMsg]
29      set rMsg [Send $recvID $sMsg $sBytes]                               ;# S5
30      binary scan $rMsg i1i1 fromWhom rBytes
31      if { $rBytes == -1} {
32          puts stdout [format "%s: cannot send to receiver" $myName]
33          break
34          }
35
36      binary scan $rMsg x8i1 inNumber                                     ;# S6
37      puts stdout [format "out number = %d in number = %d"\
38          $outNumber $inNumber]
39      }
40
41  name_detach                                                             ;# S7
42  exit
```

line 3 Invoke the Tcl interpreter.

line 6 Set unique SIMPL name.

lines 7-8 Include SIMPL library package.

lines 11-15 The program performs a ***name_attach***. Recall that this is required prior to any other SIMPL library calls. The argument in then ***name_attach*** call is the SIMPL name chosen to be unique on the local host. Again, recall the phone book analogy; this is like adding the receiver's name to the phone book.

lines 18-23 The sender needs to name locate the receiver program so the various FIFO and shared memory connections can be made. In our phone book analogy this is the same as looking up the phone number in the phone book.

lines 26-39 A loop of ten iterations is run which sends the numbers 1-10 to the receiver, retrieves a reply from the receiver in the form of the square of the sent number and then prints the sent and replied numbers to stdout.

lines 29 The ***Send*** call is the mechanism for sending out the number to be squared and retrieving the result from the receiver. The first argument represents the receiver's SIMPL ID which was gotten from the earlier ***name_locate*** call, the second argument is a pointer to the memory containing the number to be sent to the receiver, the third argument is the size in bytes of the second argument. The procedure returns the replied message.

lines 30-38 The reply message is extracted and displayed.

line 41 The SIMPL program components are removed.

4.2.3 What's In a Name?

Suppose that you wanted all of the senders above to be able to send to one of the receivers at the same time. This is actually what SIMPL is normally all about. For the sake of illustration let's use the Tcl receiver. Its SIMPL name is *receiver*. We want to run the Tcl, Python, and 'C' senders at the same time. The problem is that in the sample code they all have the same hard-coded SIMPL name, namely *sender*. We know that SIMPL names must be unique per host. No problem here, we simply change each program's SIMPL name to something different. For example, set the SIMPL names to T_sender, P_sender, and C_sender for the Tcl, Python, and 'C' sending programs respectively. Now all of the sender programs can be run simultaneously and communicate with whichever receiver program desired.

The receiver programs as they stand would be in conflict with their SIMPL names if they were to be run together. If their hard-coded names were changed to make them unique, the senders could then choose which receiver they would send their message to. Most often SIMPL programmers don't hard-code SIMPL names. They elect instead to have the SIMPL name passed into the program via the command line interface. For SIMPL senders, both its own name and the name of the receiver would be command line parameters.

Let's take a look at an example of how this might work. Suppose that we want to have the python sender program to be able to send its message to any of the three receiver programs. The three receiver programs could take their unique SIMPL names from the command line. Let's call the Tcl, Python, and 'C' receivers T_receiver, P_receiver, and C_receiver respectively. We could use a shell script to automate the startup of our various programs. Such a script might look like the following:

Startup Script

```
1   # Startup Script: program called startup
2
3   #! /usr/bin/bash
4
5   # start the Tcl receiver program
6   /usr/bin/wish tcl_receiver.tcl T_receiver &
7
8   # start the Python receiver program
9   /usr/bin/python python_receiver.py P_receiver &
10
11  # start the 'C' receiver program
12  c_receiver C_receiver &
13
14  # start the Python sender program
15  /usr/bin/python python_sender.py $1
```

line 3 Invoke the Shell interpreter.

line 6 Invoke the Tcl interpreter to run the tcl_receiver.tcl script in the background. Note the string *T_receiver* on the command line. This will be the SIMPL name of the tcl_receiver.tcl program.

line 9 Invoke the Python interpreter to run the python_receiver.py script in the background. Note the string *P_receiver* on the command line. This will be the SIMPL name of the python_receiver.py program.

line 12 Run the c_receiver binary in the background. Note the string *C_receiver* on the command line. This will be the SIMPL name of the c_receiver program.

line 15 Invoke the python interpreter to run the python_sender.py script in the foreground. Note the *$1* on the command line. This will be how we would pass the name of the receiver we want python_sender.py to send its message to. Observe the following list of possibilities:

1. *startup T_receiver* would have the python_sender.py program send its message to tcl_receiver.tcl.

2. *startup P_receiver* would have the python_sender.py program send its message to python_receiver.py.

3. *startup C_receiver* would have the python_sender.py program send its message to c_receiver.

4.3   Return Codes

We note in section 4.2 that the various SIMPL library function calls had return values. In all of these cases a -1 represents a failure of some sort. Another SIMPL library function was used to provide a string representation of an error condition in the same way that strerror(errno) might be used; the name of this function is **whatsMyError**.

In the case of the receiver program in section 4.2, the only possible fatal error resulting in a program exit was related the **name_attach** call. This is fatal because without a **name_attach** no further processing is possible. But note the **Receive** and **Reply** calls, both simply continue in the loop in the case of a failure. The failure might simply have to do with one sender program and if the receiver exits, then no other sender will be able to find it.

In the case of the sender program, all failures were considered fatal because there would be no need to carry on after that point in the case of an error. SIMPL errors should be treated by the programs using SIMPL on a case by case basis. If a sender program becomes unreachable between the receiver receiving the message and the reply being sent back, an error on the reply will occur. This does not indicate a failure in the receiver's situation; the problem may have occurred due to a dropped line between a remote sender and a local receiver for example.

See appendices B and H for more detailed information.

4.3.1   Warnings and Errors

Core SIMPL functions report errors via return codes. It is up to the user to flag and deal with them in an expedient fashion. However, SIMPL does little more than return a -1 indicating a problem. Warnings and errors which are internal to SIMPL are date and time stamped and written to a rolling log file. This file has a maximum size of 100KB. If this size is exceeded, the file is simply written over and started again. It is often a good place to look for clues to problems. Currently, this file is called *simpl* and lives in the */var/tmp* directory on a Linux-based system.

4.4   Security

The only aspect of messaging that is of interest to SIMPL is the size of the message, *period*. On a number of occasions, as the SIMPL project matured, suggestions were make to add encryption and various security measures to the core of SIMPL. We've resisted because it is our belief that this is the wrong layer in which to put security measures. The SIMPL application developer is always able to design an algorithm which would build a message, encrypt it, send it, receive it, decrypt it and then carry on with business. In this way the encryption algorithm is entirely in the application layer. Moreover, there is no form of sniffing embedded within SIMPL. If one needed to sniff messages, there are far better ways to do it.

Finally, there is a veracity issue here. SIMPL is as advertised. The code is fully open for all to inspect. There are no back doors buried in SIMPL that reports your messages to any outside party. If such a thing gets added by a third party, it goes against the express wishes of the authors and has been done utterly without their consent. The mainline SIMPL software available on the website is secure from any of this sort of tampering. If back doors exist on someone's system then they have been added after the fact.

4.5   Installing SIMPL

By this point you may be anxious to try out some things with SIMPL. Appendix A describes how to get started. There is also lots of valuable information on the main SIMPL website[3] along with helpful persons on the SIMPL mailing list.

4.6   Summary

The core SIMPL library can be summarized as:

- A very clean API of five main functions: *name_attach*, *name_locate*, *Send*, *Receive*, and *Reply*.

- A sandbox coordinated by the FIFO_PATH environment variable where all the FIFOs responsible for message synchronization actually reside.

4.7   Next Chapter

In the next chapter we are going to take a look at the messages that are sent between programs using SIMPL. In particular, we are going to examine what is known as tokenized message passing and how it is used to make a clean and functional interface between sending and receiving programs.

---

[3]The main SIMPL website is at: **http://www.icanprogram.com/simpl**.

Chapter 5

Tokenized Messages

When the first dedicated wordprocessor machines were introduced they looked something like a modern PC with a CPU box, a keyboard, and a monitor screen. Unlike our modern word processor packages, the software on these machines came on and ran from a series of floppy diskettes. Along with each diskette came a set of cardboard templates which you could lay down over your keyboard function keyset. The template had holes where the keys could poke through and relabelled each of the keys in a more friendly way for the particular piece of wordprocessing software that was running.

If the function keys on that old dedicated wordprocessor keyboard are the analogue to bytes in our SIMPL message, tokenized messages are the software analogue of that cardboard template.

Tokenized messages are one of the most powerful message formats. They are widely used because they are also one of the simplest.

We can view a SIMPL message as simply a contiguous collection of bytes (see Figure 5.1). Similarly, messaging in SIMPL terms is nothing other than a fancy way of saying:

carry some bytes with an agreed upon structure from one process to another.

Imagine this collection of bytes is divided into two parts. The first field of bytes which is of fixed length is always present in every message and when taken together, these bytes represent a unique message identifier called a token. In Figure 5.1 the token is a single binary word and can take on two values **0xfc00** and **0xfc01**. The balance of the message (which can be of variable length) represents the token context-sensitive data. In one case three integer fields and

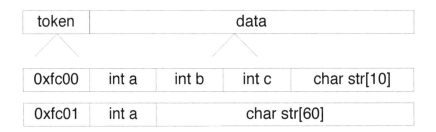

Figure 5.1: SIMPL Tokenized Message

a string of 10 characters, and in the second case a single integer and a string of 60 characters. When two processes wish to exchange such messages they simply agree on a token scheme and on the format for each tokenized message they want to exchange. To the SIMPL interprocess message transport layer all this is still just a contiguous collection of bytes. ie. SIMPL transports the messages, the applications compose and interpret them.

If two processes exchanged a fixed structure of data we wouldn't need to bother tokenizing our message. Both processes would agree on the message format and we'd be done. However, it is a rare software problem that can be decomposed into a single data structure (or if you attempt this the structure rapidly becomes unwieldy). Furthermore, most software is extended as new features are added. This is where tokenized messaging really shines. Tokenized messaging is a software framework which when applied to a contiguous block of bytes, promotes code reuse and code extendability.

In the rest of this chapter we are going to illustrate the concept of tokenized messaging using examples in the 'C' language. While the concept of a tokenized message lends itself particularly well to that language, as a concept, tokenized messaging is by no means restricted to 'C'. SIMPL developers regularly construct, exchange and decompose tokenized messages in Tcl and Python, the other principal languages with which SIMPL modules are created.

Most 'C' programmers are familiar with the basic data types, eg. int, char, or float. Fortunately, the 'C' language allows for the creation of new and complex data types. In 'C' we create new data types using a **typedef struct** statement.

The simplest form of a token field is a single integer constant. The 'C' language allows us to create enumerated lists of constants using the **typedef enum** statement.

The combination of enum and struct typedefs turn out to be exactly what is required to create an extendable tokenized message framework for SIMPL.

The code snip below illustrates these 'C' constructs applied to tokenized messaging.

```
// fun.h

#ifndef _FUN_DEF
#define _FUN_DEF

// possible token values
typedef enum
   {
   FUN_THE_QUESTION,
   MAX_NUM_FUN_TOKENS
   } FUN_TOKEN;

// create the message template
typedef struct
   {
   FUN_TOKEN token;
   char question[128];
   }MY_FUN_MSG;

_ALLOC char inArea[1024];
_ALLOC char outArea[1024];

#endif
```

We have done several things in this code snip. Firstly, we have invented a new data type which we are going to call **MY_FUN_MSG**. The **typedef struct** block tells the 'C' compiler how we want our new data type to be laid out in memory. The **typedef struct** doesn't actually allocate any memory (think of that cardboard template). The second thing we have done is create an enumerated list of tokens for our message. We have used the **typedef enum** block to arrange that list with **FUN_THE_QUESTION** being the first in that list. The third thing we have done is to allocate a couple contiguous blocks of 1K size to act as our actual SIMPL messages: inArea and outArea.

The key to understanding the power of tokenized messaging rests in the next statement:

We will never actually allocate our new data type ... we will
just declare a pointer of that type and then point it at an
arbitrary block of memory.

The code snips below illustrates how our new data type is used as a tokenized
message.

```
/*==============================================
 *
 * fun.c
 *
 * Source file for tokenized sender
 * SIMPL book
 *
 *==============================================*/

#include <stdio.h>

#define _ALLOC
#include "fun.h"
#undef _ALLOC

#include "simpl.h"

int main(int argc, char **argv )
{
int recvID;
MY_FUN_MSG *outMsg;

name_attach("SENDER",NULL);

recvID = name_locate("RECEIVER");

// map a pointer to message are memory
outMsg = (MY_FUN_MSG *)outArea;

outMsg->token = FUN_THE_QUESTION;
sprintf(outMsg->question,
  "What is the answer to life, the universe and everything ?");
Send(recvID, outArea, inArea, sizeof(MY_FUN_MSG), 1024);

name_detach();
}// end main

/*==============================================
 *
 * funrecv.c
```

```
 *
 *  Source file for tokenized receiver
 *  SIMPL book
 *
 *═══════════════════════════════════════*/

#include <stdio.h>

#define _ALLOC extern
#include "fun.h"
#undef _ALLOC

#include "simpl.h"

/*═══════════════════════════════
   funrecv − entry point
 *═══════════════════════════*/
int main(int argc, char **argv )
{
char *fromWhom;
int rbytes;
FUN_TOKEN *token;

name_attach("RECEIVER",NULL);

rbytes = Receive(&fromWhom, inArea, 1024);

// extract token value from message area memory
token = (FUN_TOKEN *)inArea;

switch(*token)
   {
   case FUN_THE_QUESTION:
      {
      MY_FUN_MSG *inMsg;

      inMsg = (MY_FUN_MSG *)inArea;

      // display the contents of this structure
      printf("token=%d\n", inMsg->token);
      printf("question=<%s>\n",inMsg->question);

      Reply(fromWhom,NULL,0);
      }
      break;
```

```
    default:
      break;
  }

name_detach();
} // end of funrecv
```

Notice that in both the sender and the receiver the **MY_FUN_MSG** structure is never used to declare a variable. It is used to declare a pointer which is then mapped onto a contiguous block of memory. The other thing to notice is that the SIMPL API functions (***Send***() and ***Receive***()) only deal with the contiguous chunks of memory (inArea and outArea) and never with the tokenized message structure itself. This separation of duty is what leads to all the power in the SIMPL tokenized messaging.

Just like in the cardboard example, there are two steps required in deploying a tokenized message:

- first you need to actually design and create it (or at least unwrap it from the box) - the typedef struct part,

- secondly you need to lay it down over the function keys - the pointer declaration and pointer instantiation parts.

This code snip forms the basic framework for all SIMPL modules which are written in 'C' and use tokenized messaging.

In our little example so far our messages have been trivial and have only flowed in one direction. In this simple world we could have gotten away without tokens. Unfortunately, the real world wants us to be much more complicated.

What would happen if we wanted to exchange a response? Here is where tokens begin to shine. Inside our **fun.h** header file we would simply add a new token (**FUN_THE_ANSWER**) to our enum:

```
// allowed token values
typedef enum
  {
  FUN_THE_QUESTION,
  FUN_THE_ANSWER,
  MAX_NUM_FUN_TOKENS
  } FUN_TOKEN;
```

and also in fun.h, a new response message structure (**MY_ANSWER_MSG**):

```
// message template
typedef struct
   {
   FUN_TOKEN token;
   int answer;
   }MY_ANSWER_MSG;
```

Inside our receiver application we would extend our **FUN_THE_QUESTION** block:

```
// from the receiver switch
case FUN_THE_QUESTION:
    {
    MY_FUN_MSG *inMsg;
    MY_ANSWER_MSG *replyMsg

    inMsg = (MY_FUN_MSG *)inArea;
    replyMsg = (MY_ANSWER_MSG *)outArea;

    // display the contents of this structure
    printf("token=%d\n", inMsg->token);
    printf("question=<%s>\n",inMsg->question);

    // compose the response
    replyMsg->token = FUN_THE_ANSWER;
    replyMsg->answer = 42;

    Reply(fromWhom,outArea, sizeof(MY_ANSWER_MSG));
    }
    break;
```

Similarly in the sender we might add the switch sequence:

```
outMsg = (MY_FUN_MSG *)outArea;
outMsg->token=FUN_THE_QUESTION;
sprintf(outMsg->question,
  "What is the answer to life, the universe and everything ?");
Send(recvID, outArea, inArea, sizeof(MY_FUN_MSG), 1024);

token=(FUN_TOKEN *)inArea;

// receiver switch dealing with each token
switch(*token)
   {
   case FUN_THE_ANSWER:
     {
```

```
    MY_ANSWER_MSG *inMsg;

    inMsg = (MY_ANSWER_MSG *)inArea;

    // display the contents of this structure
    printf("token=%d\n", inMsg->token);
    printf("answer=<%d>\n",inMsg->answer);
    }
    break;

  default:
    break;
  }
```

Note what has happened here. With a very few lines of highly recipe code, we have added bidirectional messages to our sender-receiver pair. While these messages are carried in the generic 1K buffers, they have completely different structures. The operative word is **EXTENDABLE**. Extendable is the most valuable attribute to a piece of *real world* software bar-none. The extendability of tokenized messages in Tcl or Python is almost as straightforward, even though neither of those languages supports the concept of an enum or a structure. In Tcl, for example, the enum becomes and explicit list of constants and the structure becomes a format string for a **binary scan** or **binary format** statement.

If we wanted to extend our code here by creating a completely new feature to our receiver all we would have to do is:

- modify the enum to add a new token,

- add a new message template,

- add a new case statement in the receiver switch,

- recompile and run.

We'd have to arrange for the existing sender (or a completely new sender) to compose and send our new message. More importantly the probability of breaking existing receiver code with this change is very low because each token is handled in a separate isolated code block. The KISS (Keep It Simple Stupid) philosophy is sadly a lost art amongst programmers.

5.1 Summary

SIMPL doesn't require tokenized messaging to work. It simply works much better with it.

Tokenized messaging doesn't require the 'C' language, it is just a natural fit with that language. Tokenized messaging can readily be accommodated in Tcl and Python, the other two languages used to create SIMPL modules.

The biggest advantage of tokenized messaging in SIMPL applications is their enhanced extensibility.

5.2 Next Chapter

In the next chapter we are going to take a look at the SIMPL public softwareIC repository. This repository forms the seed code for most new SIMPL users' private code repository. The code in this repository uses tokenized messaging extensively so it also forms a great set of examples for what was discussed in this chapter.

Chapter 6

SoftwareICs: Practice

We have already introduced the concept of a softwareIC and why that concept offers software designers a better way to encapsulate complexity. The SIMPL project maintains a public softwareICs repository on the website. In most cases the softwareIC code in the repository represents framework code from which a developer would customize the application specific softwareIC. The degree to which customization is required depends on the specific softwareIC and ranges from header file tweeks to addition of custom algorithm logic. All the code in the repository is accompanied by working examples of simple implementations complete with full SIMPL testing frameworks. As such this public repository is also a great starting place for new developers to SIMPL to pull seed code from for their own private repositories. In this chapter we will be discussing the softwareICs in the public repository in more detail. You can follow along by first installing the public repository code according to the procedure described in Appendix A.

While all the working examples in the repository are written in 'C', there is no reason that they could not be rewritten in Python or Tcl/Tk. As for the softwareICs themselves they are also written in 'C'. In most cases, while they could be recreated in Python or Tcl/Tk, there is little advantage to doing so.

The most basic SIMPL processes types are:

senders - those processes who compose messages and wait for replies

receivers - those processes who wait for messages and compose replies

All the building blocks discussed in this section will be composites or special types of these two basic building elements.

Over the years, as SIMPL developers, we have adopted a style for SIMPL figures, of which there are several in this chapter. The entire picture represents the SIMPL application. Within that picture the major boxes represent the SIMPL modules associated with the SIMPL application. Within those modules the **S** or **R** denote the ***Send*** or ***Receive*** ports for that module. The direction of the arrowed line represents the major data flow direction for the SIMPL message.

6.1   Simulator

One of the great advantages of the SIMPL paradigm is that is allows for the ready development of testing stubs. We have adopted the following naming convention with respect to these testing stub processes.

stub - small program that contains the essential aspects of a SIMPL sender or a receiver.

simulator - the stub for a receiver process (*sim* for short).

stimulator - the stub for a sender process (*stim* for short).

A typical simulator setup might look like Figure 6.1:

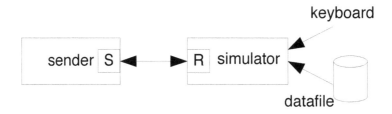

Figure 6.1: Simulator

The item being tested here is the sender. Provided that the simulator conforms to the SIMPL naming convention expected by the sender and conforms to all the expected message formats that the sender can exchange.

The sender will not be able to detect that it is talking to a test stub.

Why is this different than employing stubs in non-SIMPL designs? For one thing the stub and the SIMPL module being tested are separate executables. This means that the stub and the SIMPL module could be written in a different language. It may take less developer resources to create a test stub in Python or Tcl/Tk than the equivalent in 'C'. A 'C' based sender cannot detect that it is talking to a Tcl/Tk simulator. Since the stub is a separate executable it can be changed and enhanced without the possibility of damaging the integrity of the code under test. In fact the entire sender module can be vigorously tested in a realistic test environment without having to alter the final deployed executable in any fashion. There is no need for conditional compiles, test flags or custom code blocks that are typical of unit test scenarios in non-SIMPL designs. Once tested, the sender executable can be deployed as is, even on another network node.

The exact composition of the simulator code is highly dependent on the application. Figure 6.1 above illustrates a typical scenario whereby the simulator is exercised manually via keyboard commands. In cases where it is impractical to enter canned responses manually those are being fed in from a datafile. We have utilized more sophisticated simulators where the whole test is sequenced, controlled and driven from that data file.

6.2 Stimulator

When the object needing unit testing is a receiver one would typically use a stimulator to pretend to be the real sender in the test phase.[1]

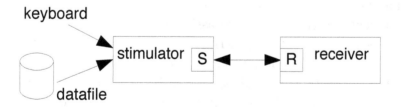

Figure 6.2: Stimulator

The item being tested here is the receiver. As was the case with the simulators above the key here is that provided that the stimulator conforms to all messaging

---

[1]The reader must exercise care as the word **stimulator** and **simulator** differ by a single letter but they represent very different test stubs.

and naming conventions the receiver process will have no way of knowing that
it is being sent a message from a stimulator as opposed to the real sender in the
final application.

> **The receiver will not be able to detect that it is talking to
> a test stub.**

As was the case with the sender process in the simulator example the receiver
under test here can be the final deployable executable in all respects. Once again
no conditional compilation or other executable altering techniques are required
in the SIMPL paradigm. The stimulator could be written in a language different
from the receiver under test. If in the real application the receiver gets messages
from multiple senders, a single stimulator could pretend to be all those senders.

As with the simulator, the sample stimulator contains a keyboard interface
for the tester to interact with. More sophisticated stimulators may feed the test
input from a data file.

6.3   Relay

In a SIMPL system all processes are named. A sender has to know the SIMPL
name of the receiver in order to open a communication channel with the
name_locate call. SIMPL contains no built in name sharing mechanism. The
application developer has to create a scheme for sharing names between modules which will communicate with each other. In the very simplest of systems
these SIMPL names can be hard coded. While this works for sample code, in
most SIMPL applications the names are assigned to processes (and passed to
other processes) as part of a startup script. The sample code in the SIMPL
softwareICs repository uses this name sharing mechanism.

There are times when this manual passing of SIMPL names becomes cumbersome to manage efficiently. In those instances it is better to architect the
SIMPL application with a single *well known* portal process to which all senders
name locate. ie. the true intended receiver's SIMPL name is *hidden* from the
sender.

An example might be an application where a GUI configurator module (receiver) is started and stopped throughout the period that the entire application
is active. Another example might be where a customized trace logger (receiver)
is dynamically started after the main application has started. Yet another example might be where the application wants to manage alternate logic through

a network outage. In all these cases a relay based portal (Figure 6.3) would be a solution.

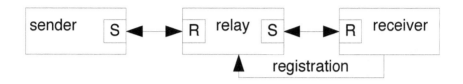

Figure 6.3: Relay

All the SIMPL application logic in Figure 6.3 is contained in the sender and the receiver. Algorithmically they behave exactly as if they were a SIMPL sender-receiver pair and the relay didn't exist.[2] While Figure 6.3 illustrates the relay with a single sender, there is no reason that there couldn't be multiple senders communicating with the single receiver via the relay.

The actual code associated with the sender does not need to change in any way to accommodate the relay. This means that the sender can be unit tested against a receiver and then deployed without change in an application which uses a relay. The sender thinks that the relay process is the intended receiver for its messages. It does all the normal name locate and send operations with the relay as if it were the final processor of the message. As such the sender needs to know the SIMPL name of the relay but does not need to know the SIMPL name of the receiver. The sample code in the repository contains a 'C' based sender. Python or Tcl/Tk could have been used to create the sender which in turn interfaced with the 'C' based relay softwareIC.

The receiver on the other hand, needs to inform the relay that it exists in order for the relay to store and forward messages to it. As such the receiver needs to know the SIMPL name of the relay. To perform this *inform the relay* step the relay construct utilizes a special tokenized SIMPL message with the REGISTRATION token. As part of the initialization sequence the receiver needs to become a temporary sender, open a communication channel to the relay and send it a REGISTRATION message broadcasting its SIMPL name. Once this registration is accomplished the receiver resumes its normal receive loop and responds to incoming messages in the normal manner. Hence the receiver code

---

[2]There is relay example code in the SIMPL SoftwareICs repository which can be installed according to the procedure in Appendix A

does need to be changed to accommodate the relay. However, those changes are
relegated to the initialization section of the code and not the **Receive-Reply**
algorithm section. As with the sender, the example code for the receiver in the
repository is 'C' based. It could have been written in Python or Tcl/Tk.

Upon receiving the REGISTRATION message the relay opens a communication channel to the receiver by doing a name locate with the supplied name
so that it can store and forward any messages. Because the relay intercepts
and handles the REGISTRATION message internally the namespace associated
with the application's messaging protocol needs to be adjusted accordingly. The
sample relay code in the repository uses a basic 16 bit word as the token in
a tokenized message passing protocol. To accommodate the possibility of a
registration and error token the namespace is expanded to include two new tokens: RELAY_REGISTER and RELAY_ERROR. In the repository example the
sender and receiver exchange a TEST tokenized message. When the sender issues a TEST message the relay process simply copies it through to the registered
receiver process and the application behaves as if the relay didn't exist. REG-
ISTER and ERROR tokens are intercepted and handled by the relay construct
itself.

The relay will incur a performance penalty over the straight sender-receiver
message exchange but the advantages which come with the construct often out-
weigh the downside. The relay is a powerful SIMPL construct.

6.4   Proxy

The proxy, like the relay, provides portal like SIMPL receiver name *hiding*. The
proxy differs from the relay in how the receiver *registers* and in the fact that the
proxy allows for multiple instances of a receiver to be prestarted.

An example where a proxy would be used is in a high transaction rate application such as a credit card authorization system. In such an application the
credit card terminals would represent multiple SIMPL senders all requiring the
services of a centralized processing house (SIMPL receiver). Using SIMPL one
could architect such a system without a proxy. This would allow the SIMPL receive FIFO to naturally queue all the credit card authorization requests. While
this would work, the overall performance would be governed by the single receiver's throughput. At times when the rate of credit card transactions is high,
credit card users would experience authorization delays as their request sits in
the queue waiting to be serviced. One way to speed things up would be to re-
engineer our application to dispatch each sender's request to a separate instance

of our receiver. This would minimize the waiting in the queue. However, since creating a separate instance of the receiver itself takes time and resources it would be helpful to prestart a number of receiver instances to buffer in the event of a burst in authorization requests.

The proxy softwareIC illustrated in Figure 6.4 would allow us to build such an application.

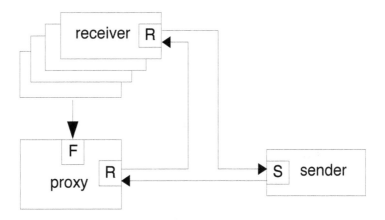

Figure 6.4: Proxy

The proxy IC makes use of intimate knowledge of the workings of SIMPL FIFOs to achieve a transparent relaying of messages from a sender to a one of the prestarted receivers.

To utilize the proxy, the sender code needs no modification over the straight sender-receiver pairing. The sender believes that the proxy is the receiver processing the messages. As such the sender only needs to know the SIMPL name of the proxy. Algorithmically the sender behaves exactly as if the message were exchanged directly with the receiver.

The receiver code must be adjusted to become proxy *aware*. As was the case in the previous relay example, the receiver needs to make itself known to the proxy. The relay used a SIMPL message for this purpose. The proxy uses a special purpose FIFO (box F in Figure 6.4) for this communication. The special purpose FIFO has two advantages over the SIMPL message:

- There is no need to *interfere* with the token namespace to accommodate proxy specific tasks like registration.

- The FIFO naturally queues prestarted instances of the receiver.

The relay used a single registration during the receiver initialization. The proxy typically re-registers each time through the transaction loop as shown by the position of the **postmyID** call in the code snip below:[3]

```
1   token=(UINT16 *)inArea;
2
3   nbytes = Receive(&sender, inArea, MAX_MSG_SIZE);
4
5   switch(*token)
6     {
7     case RELAY_TEST:
8       {
9       RELAY_TEST_MSG *inMsg;
10      RELAY_TEST_MSG *outMsg;
11
12      inMsg=(RELAY_TEST_MSG *)inArea;
13
14      outMsg=(RELAY_TEST_MSG *)outArea;
15      outMsg->token=RELAY_TEST;
16      sprintf(outMsg->str,"reply #%d",msgCount++);
17
18      Reply(sender,outArea,sizeof(RELAY_TEST_MSG));
19
20      postmyID(myID);
21      }
22      break;
```

where the **postmyID** function is essentially a **write** to the special FIFO as illustrated below:

```
1   int  postmyID(theID)
2   {
3   int  rc=-1;
4
5   rc=write(proxyID, &theID, 4);
6
7   return(rc);
8   }// end postmyID
```

There is another difference between the relay and the proxy. The relay is intimately involved in handing the SIMPL message and the SIMPL response in a store and forward manner. The proxy on the other hand, utilizes the SIMPL API **Relay** command to reroute the incoming message directly to the

---

[3]There is a full proxy example in the softwareICs repository which can be installed using the procedure in Appendix A

intended receiver without actually doing a store and forward. As such the proxy is more efficient and is not involved in the reply portion of the message exchange. This proxy mechanism has several advantages, but it means that the proxy is restricted to having its prestarted receivers on the same network node as the proxy itself resides. For most applications where the proxy would be deployed this is not a severe restriction.

6.5   Courier

Occasionally it is necessary in a design for two SIMPL receiver processes to exchange messages. A typical example would involve a user interface (UI) process. User interface processes, be they simple text based screens or GUI's, are event driven. As such they are natural SIMPL receiver type processes. They can handle incoming messages easily. However, most user interfaces dispatch outgoing requests as well. The most straightforward way to dispatch a message with SIMPL is to send it. However the **Send** in SIMPL is a blocking call. If you went ahead and coded a blocking **Send** into the UI and the receiver was busy, the interface could appear to *freeze* while the request was awaiting service. This is not the desired behaviour.

How then does a user interface (UI) get information from another SIMPL receiver? The courier construct illustrated in Figure 6.5 is a good way to accommodate this requirement.

Figure 6.5: Courier

Let us assume that in Figure 6.5 receiver1 represents the GUI and receiver2 represents the SIMPL process that the user wants information from. ie. receiver1 initiates the SIMPL message and receiver2 processes it.

Receiver2 needs no modifications to accommodate the courier.

Receiver1 (the UI in our example) does need some modifications to be made courier aware. The first modification involves manoeuvering the courier into a

reply blocked state. When the courier process is started the first thing it does
is locate the UI process it is designated to service. Once located, the courier
will send a registration type message to that process indicating that it is ready
for action. The UI process will simply note that the courier is available and not
reply, thereby leaving the courier reply blocked.

The second modification involves dispatching an outgoing request to the re-
ceiver2 process by composing and replying a message to that blocked courier.
Because **Reply** is a non-blocking call, there is no chance that this will result in
the UI *freezing* as might be the case if a blocking call was used. The courier is
now free to forward the message to the receiver2 process using a blocking **Send**.
At this point the courier is reply blocked on receiver2 and the UI is completely
free to do other things as permitted by its logic.

When receiver2 finishes processing the message it replies to the courier. The
courier simply forwards that reply on to the UI process using a blocking **Send**
and once again becomes reply blocked on the UI. ie. returns to its original state.
The UI receives this message in the normal manner, notes that it came via the
courier, marks that the courier is once again available and processes the message
in accordance with the logic coded.

The simple courier described above is the variation stored in the SIMPL
softwareICs repository. It is a single request version. If a second UI request
intended for the receiver2 process is generated within the UI before the courier
returns its first response, that request will be refused citing the *busy courier*.
A simple enhancement to this single request logic is to have a single message
queuing capability in the UI. The *busy courier* response then would only come
if a third UI request is attempted before the original response is received. In
most UI processes this single message queue is more than adequate. A larger
queue depth algorithm could be constructed readily, but the need for this is often
indicative of a poor UI design elsewhere.

Another variation on the courier model is to have a parent process fork the
couriers on demand. In some cases this capability is more desirable than having
the courier prestarted along with the GUI process. The web applet type GUI
applications are examples where this courier spawning technique is desirable.
Especially in user interface designs, the courier construct is a very useful SIMPL
building block indeed.

6.6 Agency

One of the advantages of SIMPL is that there is very little algorithmic difference between a receiver's **Send** driven message loop and a sender's **Reply** driven message loop. Behaviourally however, there is a fundamental difference. In the first case the receiver holds the sender blocked until the message is processed. In the second case the message initiator (the receiver) is not held while the message is processed.

In SIMPL application designs where the sender does the message processing, it is often necessary to exchange messages between two SIMPL senders. For this the agency construct illustrated in its simplest form in Figure 6.6 is used.

Figure 6.6: Agency

In Figure 6.6 the requestor is simply another name for the normal message initiator: the sender. Similarly, the agent (also a SIMPL sender) contains the logic for processing the requestor's SIMPL message, logic that normally would exist in a SIMPL receiver. Variations to this basic agency framework all have to do with the blocking logic applied to the requestor message. These variations can span the full spectrum from full blocking (as in our example) to immediate unblocking with message queuing (as in the broadcaster softwareIC example below).

The agency construct is a natural SIMPL message router. Often times different portions of the tokenized message namespace are allocated to separate SIMPL agent processes. An example of this might be a message processing stack. Each layer in the stack is handled by a separate agent.

The agency construct is also a natural gateway. Sometimes an application specification calls for the gateway to assert control on the message flow and sequencing to the agent processes. Straight SIMPL messaging is always immediate delivery with a democratic first in first out queue if the receiver is busy. Agency based gateways can introduce queuing and priority based message delivery algorithms. This agency framework forms the basis for several other softwareICs in the SIMPL repository:

- Broadcaster

- Scheduler

- Statemachine

The softwareICs we have discussed so far (stimulator, simulator, relay, proxy
and courier) all share the distinction that stock SIMPL senders and receivers
can be adapted to work with these ICs in a straightforward manner, sometimes
without any changes. The requestor, agent and agency form a much more connected package. While stock sender and receiver algorithmic logic can readily
be adapted to work as requestors and agents, the framework changes are more
fundamental. An agent cannot stand as a SIMPL process on its own. It is tightly
coupled to its agency.

As such, the agency framework makes use of what are termed wrapped
SIMPL messages. A wrapped SIMPL message is a tokenized SIMPL message
embedded inside the data area of another tokenized SIMPL message. In our
example the outer layer message is used by the agency. The inner layer message
is produced by the requestor and consumed by the agent. The requestor and the
agent build the two layer messages to route their cargo through the agency.

Other than the need for SIMPL wrapper messages, the requestor and agent
behave exactly as if the requestor were sending its message to a basic receiver. In
fact there is very little difference in the requestor code for dealing with agencies.
Why then go to all this trouble?

First of all, it is now possible to dynamically start and stop the agent process
in this system without affecting the requestor. In systems where the agent is
undergoing significant revisions or upgrades this is a distinct advantage.

Secondly, the requestor in this system does not need to know the name of
the agent in order to exchange a message with it. Like the relay and proxy, the
agency construct can be viewed as a message gateway.

To understand the further advantages, we need to examine the case where
we may have multiple requestors all talking to the same agency and agent. In
this scenario the agency will actually receive and queue the requestor's messages.
The agency logic can then be in control of the order in which these messages are
dispatched to the agent. In a normal sender/receiver pairing the FIFO imposes
a strict first in first out ordering and it is not possible to have a higher priority
message jump ahead in the queue. In the agency construct this is very possible.

In addition, in the normal SIMPL sender/receiver pairing the messaging is synchronous. It is intentionally difficult to kick a sender out of a reply blocked state other than by having the receiver do a reply. This means things like timeouts or *aged data* are difficult to handle. The agency construct makes these things relatively easy to manage. While messages are pending in the agency queue the agency can be kicked into examining these periodically for timeouts or aging.

Finally, in normal SIMPL message exchanges there is no concept of delayed, repeated or scheduled delivery. Once again the agency construct makes all these forms of message delivery possible.

The agency construct will suffer a performance penalty when compared against a basic sender/receiver pair because at least two extra messages need to be exchanged in each transaction. The agency framework however, is a powerful one and has been used in several of our projects over the years.

6.7   Broadcaster

There are times in a design where there is a need for a one to many sender/receiver relationship. An example might be a SIMPL application with multiple GUI interfaces that all need to be fed the same data. Another example might be an application which needs an audit logger for recording all message traffic to a GUI screen. For simple cases one can simply have the sender locate all the intended recipients and loop through sending to each. In more sophisticated designs the broadcaster construct illustrated in Figure 6.7 is used.

The actual application code is contained in the sender and receivers in Figure 6.7. Since this is a one to many message relationship, the actual message protocol between the sender and any receiver has to include a simple NULL reply since SIMPL has no mechanism to push multiple replies in response to a single *Send*. In cases where the broadcaster would be used this is not a severe messaging protocol restriction. During normal operation any message transmitted by the sender will get distributed to all the registered receivers (eg. receiver1,2,3 in Figure 6.7).

The broadcaster-agent and broadcaster-queue are simplified derivatives of the agent and agency construct we discussed earlier. The broadcaster-queue stores and forwards all message traffic it receives to a single broadcaster-agent process. The broadcaster-queue generates the NULL reply to all incoming messages. The broadcaster-agent maintains a list of SIMPL receivers to send to. The broadcaster-queue utilizes the same token namespace shifting technique

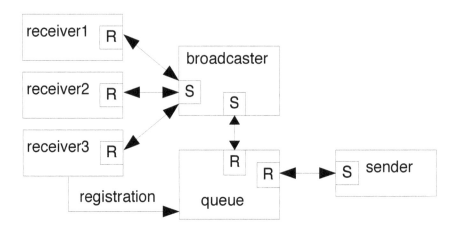

Figure 6.7: Broadcaster

employed by the relay to accommodate the broadcaster specific tokens: REGIS-
TER, DEREGISTER and WHAT_YA_GOT. This technique supplants the more
sophisticated SIMPL message wrapping technique employed by the more general
purpose agency-agent construct.

As such the sender need not be modified in any way to work with the broadcaster. The sender simply treats the broadcaster-queue as the intended receiver
of its messages. Since the expected protocol includes a NULL reply the sender
is unable to distinguish that it is dealing with a broadcaster-queue and not the
actual intended receiver(s). In fact the sender can be unit tested against those
intended receivers and then simply deployed via the broadcaster.

The receivers on the other hand, need to be broadcaster aware in much the
same way that receivers connected to a relay were relay aware. The broadcaster
needs to know the SIMPL names of the receivers it is broadcasting to. This
information is communicated via a special tokenized message using the REG-
ISTER token during the initialization sequence for the receiver. Similarly the
receiver issues the DEREGISTER token to the broadcaster at any time it no
longer wishes to receive the transmissions. The broadcaster will automatically
deregister any recipient upon a transmission failure. Outside of the registration
and deregistration sequences these receivers process messages as if they came
directly from the sender.

The WHAT_YA_GOT token is utilized internally between the broadcaster-
agent and the broadcaster-queue.

A typical sequence may start as follows. A receiver (say receiver1) decides that it wishes to receive broadcast messages. As part of that sequence it sends a registration type message to the broadcaster-queue process. This inserts this receiver into the broadcaster-agents' broadcast list. At this point the sender may send a message to the broadcaster-queue process. The broadcaster-queue will immediately acknowledge this message with a NULL reply. Each receiver in the broadcaster-agents' list will receive a copy of this message. All receiver replies will be absorbed by the broadcaster-agent. If, while the actual broadcasting is taking place, a sender transmits a new message to the broadcaster-queue that message is simply placed on the queue for later transmission.

While Figure 6.7 illustrates a broadcaster with a single sender, there is no restriction on the number of senders that can transmit messages to the broadcast-queue. For cases like the audit logger or synchronization of multiple GUI screens with the same data stream, the broadcaster construct is a powerful SIMPL softwareIC.

6.8 Scheduler

All SIMPL messages are delivered immediately subject to the democracy of the first in first out (FIFO) queuing that occurs if the receiver is busy. There are times in a design where there is a need to schedule messages for delivery at some future time. In addition, one might want that message to be scheduled regularly on a daily or weekly schedule.

Figure 6.8 illustrates a derivative of the agency which can permit scheduled delivery of SIMPL messages.

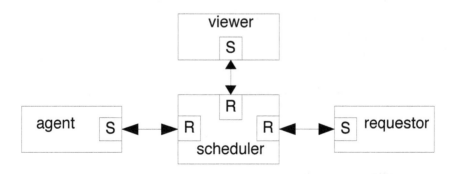

Figure 6.8: Scheduler

The requestor is the message initiator. However, since this message is going to be delivered at some future time, the messaging protocol would likely entail an immediate NULL reply to unblock the requestor. Figure 6.8 shows two agent processes: **agent** and **viewer**.

The example code contains a viewer which is a console viewer of the messages currently queued in the scheduler. Although the sample code illustrates a console process it could very well have been a SIMPL enabled GUI. The agent is the module which processes the requestors' delayed message. This agent is reply driven from the scheduler queue.

All messages in the scheduler example are tokenized. However, the requestor submits a wrapped SIMPL message. The outer portion is stripped away and used by the scheduler itself. The inner message is passed through to the agent for processing. For the sample code the contents of the outer portion are described by the **SCHEDULE_THIS_MSG** structure in the **schedulerMsgs.h** header. It contains various fields for controlling the scheduling of the inner message.

The main looping sequence in the scheduler is kicked off by the on board timer. Each click of that timer spawns the following activities:

- A check on the queued messages to mark any that have now expired.

- If the agent is available the first available expired message is dequeued and replied to the agent.

- If the dequeued message is on a daily or weekly repeat it is stamped with the next timestamp and left on the queue.

The message to be delivered to the agent is treated as a package of bytes by the scheduler, to be queued until the time comes to forward it on the agent. The agent in this scheme only sees this package of bytes with all the scheduling info stripped away before it is forwarded. Obviously, in the interest of simplicity this example scheduler lacks some features, that could readily be added such as:

- Text (or XML) file driven input of the scheduled message.

- Some form of persistent storage of the schedule queue in the event of a restart.

- Management functionality in addition to viewing the queue such as selecting and deleting messages.

Nevertheless, the scheduler framework in the repository is a very usable softwareIC.

6.9 Statemachine

Another derivative of the agency in the repository is the statemachine soft-wareIC. State machine logic is a very common element of many software applications. State machines are by definition very customized to the problem they are trying to represent. As such it is very difficult to build a general purpose state machine that works for many classes of problems. Instead this softwareIC takes the approach of a source code framework.

The **SM_common** directory contains the basic state machine infrastructure and a definition of an API to that infrastructure.

The **SM_door** subdirectory contains the specific state machine logic and implementations of the state machine API for a very simple four state door (Figure 6.9).

These two source code sections are re-merged by the Makefile into a single executable. The idea is that for another type of system the **SM_common** stays and the **SM_whatever** is created which results in a new type of executable. In this manner the **SM_common** code can be shared across several different executables.

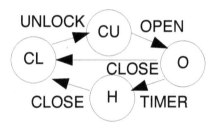

Figure 6.9: Door

Where the states are:

CL - closed and locked

CU - closed and unlocked

O - opened

H - held open

The events in this simple door system are:

UNLOCK - key is turned to unlock the door

OPEN - door is pulled open

CLOSE - door is shut (and automatically relocked)

TIMER - held open timer expires

The sample door illustrated in Figure 6.9 operates in the following manner. With the door in a closed locked state (CL) a resident steps up and inserts a key to unlock the door. This causes our door to transition to the closed unlocked (CU) state. If the resident pulls open the door, breaking a contact sensor, the the door transitions to an open (O) state. At this point a timer is engaged to monitor the length of time the door is left open. If the resident allows the door to close the door state transitions back to closed locked (CL) and the timer is cancelled. If the timer expires first the door transitions to a held (H) state and an alarm message is triggered. When the door is finally closed the alarm is cancelled and the door returns to a closed locked (CL) state.

The sample code in the repository is represented in Figure 6.10 below:

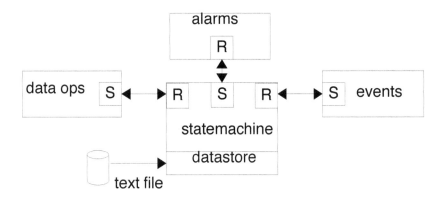

Figure 6.10: Statemachine

The datastore in the sample code is a doubly linked in memory list, but it could easily be substituted by any number of more sophisticated datastores as the application requires. The datastore itself is fed from a simple **tag, value** paired text file. To make this datastore more embedded friendly we have employed the concept of a single block of dynamically allocated memory which is then subdivided into memory pools. The datastore is organized with a separate record for each door. The complete state of a given door is stored in this record so the **statemachine** logic can accommodate a number of doors in a single SIMPL module.

The main **statemachine** is for the most part a SIMPL receiver, but occasionally a SIMPL sender. On the receive port this **statemachine** can accommodate two classes of messages:

- Those associated with operating on the datastore.

  - **ADD**
  - **DELETE**
  - **OVERWRITE**
  - **RESYNC**

- The events themselves.

In the sample code a single test stub called **eventStim** is involved in issuing all these messages via a simple command line interface.

The **eventStim** is also configured to receive any **ALARM** messages that the **statemachine** issues, which in the case of our simple door is associated with the door being held open beyond a specified time window.

6.10 Polling Emitter

SIMPL is often used in low speed (less than 100 samples per second) data acquisition/control applications such as building automation. This by definition means that in such an application at least one SIMPL module will be interfacing with hardware to gather and transmit data. If that hardware interface is a serial connection, one class of data acquisition/control application which still finds usage involves polling the serial interfaced hardware. In such cases the SIMPL interfacing module must reconcile the need to poll the serial port, accept occasional data for transmission on that serial port and emit the occasional SIMPL message containing acquired data. The first and last requirement make this process a natural SIMPL sender. The second requirement wants this process to be an occasional receiver.

The polling emitter illustrated in Figure 6.11 tries to square away these conflicting requirements associated with this class of application. This softwareIC solves this problem by making the Polling Emitter an occasional sender while allowing for a small piece of shared memory be used to intercept the polling loop and trigger a *call home* response from the emitter.

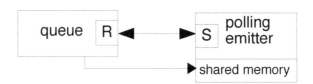

Figure 6.11: Polling Emitter

In the 6.11 we are showing the emitter connected to a queuing receiver process. While this is strictly not necessary one will want to take care that all
messages sent from the polling emitter are blocked for the minimum amount of
time.

A typical sequence may start as follows. The queue and the emitter are
started up. The emitter name locates the queue and sends an initialization
message indicating to the queue where the shared memory block is. The queue
process will reply back to unblock the emitter and establish a connection to the
emitter's shared memory.

While this shared memory could contain any structured data which the queue
and the emitter agree upon. eg. a table of serial devices which are to be polled.
We are going to restrict this example to the simplest of configurations where the
shared memory contains a single *call home* flag. The queue process will be the
changer of this flag and the emitter process will only read it.

Inside the emitter there is a loop which is endlessly cycling around all the
hardware it is supposed to be polling. The sample code in the repository uses a
one second interval checking on a text file to simulate a polling loop. If a change
has been made to that text file, the sample code will reread the file and send its
contents on to the queue.

Each pass through that loop we are going to have the emitter check on the flag
located in the shared memory area. If that flag is set we are going to interrupt
the polling and send a CALL_HOME tokenized message to the queue process.
This gives the queue process an opportunity to stuff something into the reply
and then clear the flag.

In this manner we can demonstrate the polling emitter looping around checking on the simulated hardware (a file) and emitting any changes that it observes
in that simulated hardware. We can interupt the polling loop at any time and
have the emitter call home to receive some data back from the queue. Presumably this would be a message destined for the hardware that the emitter is

polling.

6.11 Summary

In this chapter we have presented the SIMPL public softwareICs repository. This is an ongoing effort and changes and additions are made all the time. Most new SIMPL developers find the code in this public repository forms great seed code for their projects.

6.12 Next Chapter

In the next chapter we are going to examine how the SIMPL core library can be made network aware without having to change any code. In SIMPL terminology we refer to this type of SIMPL application as being network agnostic.

Chapter 7

Surrogates and Networking

In chapter 4 we looked at how SIMPL operates on a single host at a local level. It was mentioned that in order to operate over a network SIMPL utilizes the services of programs called *surrogates*. In this chapter we will examine the surrogate programs and their operation in greater detail as well as some issues pertaining to network communications.

7.1   Background

The overriding desire to make network transport of SIMPL messages invisible is the driving force behind the software design of networking SIMPL. On a local level, SIMPL is composed of sending and receiving programs that communicate with each other directly by passing well-defined messages in areas of shared memory. Shared memory is not normally network accessible. This should not prevent SIMPL from transparently transporting messages between nodes.

In order to make network SIMPL function in the same fashion as local SIMPL we have to address the following issues:

1. We need a scheme to replicate and synchronize data in shared memory on one node with shared memory on another node.

2. There can be any number of disparate ways (protocols) that govern the remote communications between hosts that SIMPL might use. Certainly we can think of a few immediately, but what about the future? We need a design that is amenable to extending SIMPL in concert with new and different protocols. This issue is covered below in the section called *Surrogates*.

3. We need a transparent way of name locating a remote program. That is, we want to simply pass in a name string to the **name_locate** call in the same way that we do locally. Recall that name locating is SIMPL's way of making a communication path between sender and receiver. This makes the API identical and accordingly there would be no obvious difference between local and remote SIMPL connectivity as far as the programmer using SIMPL is concerned. Moreover, if the name string passed in to the **name_locate** function is a variable, then it can be anything. The program making the **name_locate** call is then indifferent as to whether the looked for program is local or remote - which is as it should be. How this issue is dealt with is described below in detail in the section called *Remote Name Location*.

4. Given that SIMPL might use different protocols in order to communicate remotely we will need some way to decide which method of communication is desired and/or available. This issue is dealt with below in the section called *Protocol Router*.

The blocking messaging protocol that local SIMPL uses makes a transparent networked SIMPL possible.

7.2   Surrogates

Surrogates are aptly named. They are programs that invisibly replace actual senders and receivers so that SIMPL network communications appear to be local and seamless. Surrogates come in two varieties, namely senders and receivers, depending on which type of SIMPL module they are standing in for.

Suppose that a sender on one host needs to send a message to a receiver on another remote computer. To maintain a seamless API, this sender program will make a **name_locate** call seeking a connection to the remote receiver. Conceptually, if we can *arrange* for this sender to *think* that a receiver surrogate of the same name exists locally, this local SIMPL connection can be made to succeed. Similarly if we can *arrange* for the receiver to *think* that a sender surrogate is to be the origin of any messages, another local SIMPL connection can be made to succeed. Finally, if we can arrange for the surrogate pair to agree on a network protocol for inter-surrogate communication, we can use local SIMPL functions to pass messages over the resulting composite channel. What actually happens is a bit more complicated.

Firstly, via the **name_locate** call it will be ascertained if such a remote receiver exists and can be reached. If so, a surrogate receiver will be started on the computer that is running the sender program. At the same time, a surrogate sender will be started on the remote computer that is home to the remote receiver program. These two surrogate partners agree on a network protocol to be used for communication. The SIMPL name of the remote receiver is then communicated across the network to the surrogate partner (surrogate sender). Armed with this name the surrogate sender can do a local **name_locate** to complete the full communications channel from local sender to remote receiver. In this way the local sender's **name_locate** can now return a valid SIMPL local channel ID: that of the receiver surrogate. The sender can then use local SIMPL functions to send its message. The recipient of that message is a surrogate for the remote receiver. While the sender remains blocked awaiting a response, the receiver surrogate can safely transmit the contents of the message using the network protocol to its surrogate partner (the surrogate sender) on the remote node. When the surrogate sender receives the message on the network channel it simply uses a local **Send** to deliver the message to the intended receiver. The response travels back in exactly the reverse manner. As far as the original sender and receiver programs are concerned, they are communicating directly with each other. See Figure 7.1

The surrogate receiver/sender pairs communicate with each other via some sort of network communications protocol. At the time of this writing there were two such computer communications protocols in use. The first, and the most important of these is based on TCP/IP sockets. TCP/IP is the protocol for the Internet and is available on most hardware platforms as a result. As long as a host supports a TCP/IP stack and is connected in some fashion to another host with a TCP/IP stack, then SIMPL communication can occur (within security limits of course). This TCP/IP surrogate type is useful on local and wide area networks as well as the Internet.

The second method of communication is more restrictive. It employs a RS-232 communications protocol. In many wired RS-232 situations the throughput is less than Ethernet enabled TCP/IP. Similarly the effective range for RS-232 can be relatively short. However, with the advent of RS-232 radio modems this distance can be expanded to 25km wirelessly. The RS-232 surrogate protocol still has its uses. For one it can act as a failover backup for a primary TCP/IP network. For some classes of devices the restrictions associated with RS-232 are not an issue and this is an acceptable protocol for SIMPL communication. Since RS-232 is typically a point to point protocol it can be more secure than a routed TCP/IP protocol.

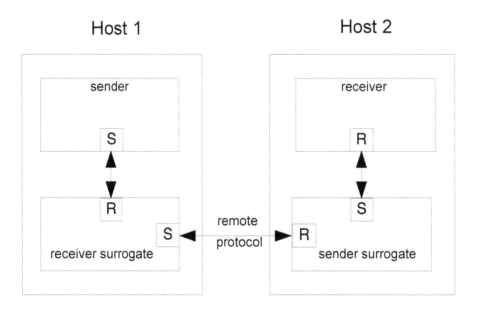

Figure 7.1: Surrogate Programs

These two surrogates follow roughly the same general framework. If one wanted to make surrogates that used a RS-422 protocol for example, it would be very straightforward to modify the current RS-232 mechanism. In some of the following sections we will explore more of the details of the TCP/IP and RS-232 approaches.

Like the core SIMPL library, the SIMPL surrogates are written in 'C' language. The surrogates themselves link to the SIMPL core library in order to function. As such we do not consider the SIMPL surrogates to be core to SIMPL. In a very real sense surrogates are merely specialized SIMPL modules. Having said this the surrogates are included in the main SIMPL package because they provide transparent networking which greatly increases SIMPL's functional applicability.

7.3   Remote Name Location

From a programmer's standpoint, the connection between a strictly local use of SIMPL (restricted to communications on one host) and remote SIMPL is the *name_locate* call. The mechanics of this function call are described in detail in Appendix B. The syntax of the *name_locate* call is unchanged between a local and a remote SIMPL call. There is still only a single name string as the functional argument. The call still returns the SIMPL ID of the local process pointed to by the SIMPL name. What varies between a local and remote call is the format of the name string. The name string that is passed into the *name_locate* function call takes the form:

protocol name:host name:process name

Note the demarcation of the three parts of the name string by colons. Only the process name portion is compulsory. The other two parts are optional. The *host name* must be specified if the sending and receiving processes are running on different host computers. The *protocol name* must be specified if there are more than one type of surrogate protocol available and the desired protocol is not running as the default.

Now, let's look at each of these values in turn. The *process name* determines the SIMPL name of the receiver that the sender wants to communicate with. This is all that has to be filled in for local SIMPL communications. Suppose that we have a sender with the SIMPL name 'Newton' that wants to send a message to a local program with the SIMPL name 'Einstein'. The Newton program would simply make the following call:

id = *name_locate*("Einstein");

Suppose now that both Newton and Einstein are running on a host computer called 'Earth'. Another variation that will also work for local name locating would be the following call:

id = *name_locate*("Earth:Einstein");

Since both Newton and Einstein are running on Earth, then the *name_locate* call would also be treated as local SIMPL communications. No surrogates will be started and local SIMPL will be used to transmit the message.

Suppose now that the Newton sender program is running on a host computer called Earth but the Einstein receiver program is running on a host called Mars. In this case, Newton would make a *name_locate* call as follows:

id = *name_locate*("Mars:Einstein");

If this call is successful a surrogate pair will be set up between Newton and Einstein. That is, Newton and a surrogate_r will be *local SIMPL connected* on Earth, Einstein and a surrogate_s will be *local SIMPL connected* on Mars and the surrogate_r and surrogate_s will be *remote SIMPL connected* via whatever protocol and hardware is the default.

If there is only one type of surrogate daemon running on the Earth host then the above *name_locate* call will be adequate. If there is more than one type of surrogate protocol available between Earth and Mars, it may be preferable to

choose the surrogate type directly rather than leave it up whatever is available
at the time of the *name_locate* call. Leaving the protocol name value vacant
is a signal that the default surrogate will do. We may choose to explicitly direct
the protocol to be TCP/IP. In this case, the Newton program will make the call
as follows:

$$\text{id} = \textit{name\_locate}(\text{"SIMPL\_TCP:Mars:Einstein"});$$

This would force the surrogates to be of type TCP/IP.

7.4   Protocol Router

The *protocol router* is a program that must always be present if remote
name_locate calls are made; the binary file name for this program is called
protocolRouter and is generally run as a background process. The purpose of
this program is to keep track of the latest available surrogate_r programs per
protocol. When surrogate daemons (surrogateTcp and/or surrogateRS232)are
started, they fork into two quite separate programs, viz. surrogate_R and sur-
rogate_S. The uppercase R and S signify that these two programs will be the
parents of the various surrogate_r and surrogate_s programs respectively. The
various surrogate_r and surrogate_s are the actual programs that provide the
remote Send/Receive/Reply mechanism by acting as surrogate pairs in the remote communication. When surrogate_R starts up it forks a surrogate_r process.
After a successful fork, surrogate_R reports the SIMPL name of the surrogate_r
process to the protocol router and the protocol router adds this SIMPL name to
an internal table.

Upon receiving a remote name locate request from a prospective sender application, protocol router checks its internal table for a surrogate_r with the correct
protocol (or in the default case the first available surrogate_r in the table) and
in the case of a match, replies the SIMPL name of the surrogate_r process.

There exists a SIMPL utility program called *dumpProtocolTable*. When run
from the command line it sends a message to the protocol router program asking
for the contents of its internal table. Upon receipt of this information, dump-
ProtocolTable displays a list of the various surrogate_r programs available. It is
run as is and takes no command line parameters. It is a good way to check that
the required surrogates are available for use.

7.4.1 Name Locate Operations

The *name_locate* call performs the following actions internally:

1. Deciphers the input string. This action identifies the nature of the communication as to whether it is local or remote. If local, then the name of the receiving process is all that is important and anything else is discarded. If remote, then the name of the receiving process and the host computer are essential. If the protocol is not present, then the default protocol will be tried.

2. If the name located process is local, then a connection is made to its trigger FIFO and we are finished. If the process is remote, then the local protocol router process is name located.

3. Once the protocol router has been name located a message is sent to it requesting the name of the next surrogate_r process with the desired protocol that is available. The protocol router provides this information in a reply message.

4. When the reply message with the necessary information, the local surrogate_r is name located and the remote name locate mesage is sent to it. The surrogate_r process then tries to make a connection to the remote host and finally to its surrogate_s partner if all goes well.

5. The surrogate_r program replies back the result of the remote name locate and the name locate function returns with the SIMPL ID of the surrogate_r process or a failure.

7.5   Surrogates and Protocols

While surrogates facilitate transparent transport of SIMPL messages between SIMPL processes on different network nodes, they also introduce complications associated with failures at the network transport layer. An ideal network transport layer would be capable of detecting and reporting network failures in a timely manner to the respective surrogates at each end. Once such a network failure is detected the challenge is to report such failures back to the actual SIMPL application in a manner consistent with the *need to know* SIMPL axiom. Recall Section 3.2 in Chapter 3.

The SIMPL sender should not need to know that a network transport layer is being used to transport SIMPL messages to the intended SIMPL receiver.

The TCP/IP surrogate is the original SIMPL surrogate and hence is widely used. TCP/IP as a network transport layer is far from ideal when it comes to detecting and reporting network or socket failures.[1]

In fact, TCP/IP cannot easily detect the loss of connectivity with a socket partner without the use of a separate heartbeat packet and a timeout. This poses immense challenges for the design of a TCP/IP surrogate. While a heartbeat/timeout combination works reasonably well for outright network failures, it can yield false positives on a sluggish TCP/IP network. Such a failure is communicated back to the SIMPL sender in an error message which is indistinguishable from a local receiver failure. If care isn't taken with the error recovery algorithm, runaway loops can result especially if the algorithm is a straight retry.

The bottom line is that while the SIMPL developer is largely isolated from the details of network transport, it is important that the developer be aware of the failure detection limitations associated with the particular network transport layer planned for the application.

7.5.1   TCP/IP Surrogate

TCP/IP surrogates were the first to be written because of the pervasiveness of these protocols. Based on a layering model that has met with success in the development of network protocols, TCP/IP allows connectivity between all sorts of computer hardware running under different operating systems and as such has made possible the Internet.

For the operational details of the TCP/IP surrogate, please refer to Appendix C.

7.5.2   RS-232 Surrogate

The RS-232 surrogates operate somewhat differently from the TCP/IP surrogates. From a remote application's point of view there is no difference of course. Because there are no sockets ultimately attached to the serial port there is only one conduit available. In this way, host one attaches to host two via one serial line. Because of the surrogates, any number of programs on host 1 may communicate with any number on host 2, however communications with any other host would require another serial line. An exception to this would be the case that a computer host communicated with a number of devices all connected to

---

[1]TCP/IP Illustrated, Volume 1 by W. Richard Stevens, Addison-Wesley Pub.,1994, ISBN 0-201-63346-9.

the same serial line. All of the devices would be privy to all communications but would be programmed to only respond to some unique identification. This would be a good example of where tokenized message passing would be valuable. Refer to Chapter 5 for more on tokenized messages.

For the operational details of the RS-232 surrogate, please refer to Appendix D.

7.5.3   tclSurrogate

The SIMPL toolkit has always been useful for constructing applications on Linux (or other UNIX like) systems. Very early on it became apparent that there was a need to construct hybrid applications where SIMPL message exchange would occur between a SIMPL process and code running on a non-UNIX like OS.

The first such hybrid application for SIMPL involved message exchanges between a Linux server running SIMPL and a Windows client running a Tcl/Tk applet. The design objective was to preserve the Send/Receive/Reply aspect of SIMPL messaging in this hybrid environment. The solution was to divide the Windows client process into two parts:

- the SIMPL messaging part

- the business logic part

These two parts were then connected using a TCP/IP socket. The tclSurrogate protocol (see Appendix E) was then used to facilitate the communication between the parts. Once this separation was envisioned it became possible to separate the SIMPL part and the business logic part on separate network nodes.

As the design progressed it became apparent that the SIMPL portion could be made entirely generic. It was designed as a forking Linux daemon which was given the name tclSurrogate. This tclSurrogate was designed to listen to port 8000 and fork a child process upon connection. This child process then became the SIMPL part of the remote application. Since the early remote applications were written in Tcl/Tk the name tclSurrogate was chosen and has stuck ever since.

To facilitate the building of Tcl/Tk applications using this tclSurrogate gateway, a Tcl/Tk package (library) was constructed. The early version of this library (fcsocket.tcl) simply exposed the raw TCP/IP tclSurrogate protocol as a series of functions. This worked well, but the resulting Tcl/Tk code did not look like the SIMPL API.

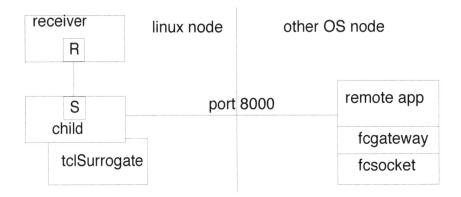

Figure 7.2: tclSurrogate

Meanwhile, work started in the SIMPL project on a Tcl/Tk shared library for SIMPL (fctclx). Here the Tcl/Tk language was extended to include the SIMPL API. The shared library was written in 'C' and hence was able to call the SIMPL core library directly. At this point Tcl/Tk standalone SIMPL applications could be written for Linux systems, ie. systems which could support the Tcl/Tk shared library. This Tcl/Tk API is described in Appendix B. At this point it was possible to write SIMPL applications in Tcl/Tk using two different approaches:

- the tclSurrogate gateway approach

- the Tcl/Tk shared library approach

However, the code did not look the same. An abstraction layer library (fcgateway) was created in Tcl/Tk to remap the Tcl/Tk shared library API calls onto the raw tclSurrogate calls. Today Tcl/Tk applications can be written to a single unified API and deployed either as a stand alone SIMPL application (Linux) or as a tclSurrogate gateway connected app (Windows).

Meanwhile the tclSurrogate protocol proved to be quite flexible. It was adapted to other hybrid SIMPL systems. One of these involved adapting this protocol to a deeply embedded network appliance.[2] This allowed for totally transparent SIMPL messaging to occur between a Linux server and this network appliance or between a standalone Tcl/Tk application and this network appliance.

---

[2]A paper describing the use of the tclSurrogate protocol for a deeply embedded network appliance is available at: http://www.hometoys.com/htinews/apr06/articles/appliance/part2.htm.

7.5.4   QNX Surrogates

A number of years ago it became necessary for SIMPL to communicate with QNX. QNX performs its network Send/Receive/Reply on the network level. At the time, only the TCP/IP surrogate existed for SIMPL. So how does one get a Linux host to talk to a QNX host at the application level? We decided to add TCP/IP surrogates to QNX. They run almost exactly the same as those on Linux but the local core Send/Receive/Reply calls used are strictly QNX's own.

The QNX version supported is 4.25 which is rather dated now so we only mention this in passing. Current versions of SIMPL still communicate with those surrogates written for QNX4.25. The QNX surrogate software is available on the SIMPL website.

7.5.5   Internal Parameters

There are a couple of internal parameters for configuring SIMPL surrogates. They are as follows:

1. Message Type. This is discussed in detail in Section 7.5.6. This has to do with the byte ordering of integers and how different computer architectures store integers in memory. If all of the networked hosts follow the same scheme then we may compile the surrogates as follows:

   make install MSG_TYPE=SUR_BIN

   This is currently the default. If on the other hand the various hosts store integers differently, the the surrogates should be compiled as follows:

   make install MSG_TYPE=SUR_CHR

2. Message Buffering. This only applies to TCP/IP surrogates and not to RS-232 surrogates. If message buffering is desired for reading and writing, it can be enforced. For message buffering the TCP/IP surrogates must be compiled with the following directive:

   make install MSG_BUFFERING=BUFFERED

   Messages are not buffered by default. The default directive for no buffering is as follows:

   make install MSG_BUFFERING=NOT_BUFFERED

7.5.6   Endian Issues

Different computer architectures may store information differently. One of these differences may be the order of storage in terms of memory addressing otherwise

AB	CD	Big Endian
CD	AB	Little Endian

Table 7.1: Endian Memory Storage of 0xABCD

known as byte ordering. Suppose by way of an example we have a short integer. This consists of two bytes. Suppose further that we have the number 43981 which is ABCD in hexadecimal. The following table shows how this number could be stored.

If a big endian host sent this integer to a little endian host, the number would appear to be CDAB or 52651 in decimal. If a little endian host sent this integer to a big endian host the number would appear also to be CDAB.

If the various hosts that are using SIMPL on a network are homogeneous, ie. they are all big endian or little endian then there is no problem. The difficulties arise when there is a mix of computer types. This was a problem within socket programming due to the heterogeneous nature of networks like the Internet. A discussion of network byte ordering is beyond the scope of this book but how it affects SIMPL is not. In terms of the Internet, big endian was chosen as the de facto standard for integer exchanges. The issue is overcome in that all integers are converted from little endian to big endian if necessary prior to communication and then turned back into little endian as the case may be. This is usually known as *host ordering to network ordering* and *network ordering to host ordering* respectively.

Networked SIMPL uses tokenized message passing between surrogates in order to identify the sorts of messages being passed. See Appendix F. These tokens are integers and so could also fall into the same difficulty between heterogeneous hosts. Rather than follow the method of converting integers from little endian to big endian and vice versa, the SIMPL internal tokens are converted to character strings prior to sending and converted back upon reception.

SIMPL currently uses the binary approach by default. If you are using SIMPL on a heterogeneous network then the surrogates must be forced to use the character string approach. For SIMPL to use the character approach the surrogate software must be compiled with the following directive:

make install MSG_TYPE=SUR_CHR

IMPORTANT: As far as SIMPL is concerned, the message content is of no interest. The nature of the content is beyond the scope of SIMPL since a message can be anything at all and its true nature is only understood by the sender and the receiver. Consequently, what happens to the message is up to the sender

Binary to Character	Character to Binary
btosUI(unsigned int n, char *s, int c)	stobUI(char *, int c)
btosSI(signed int n, char *s, int c)	stobSI(char *, int c)
btosUSI(unsigned short int n, char *s, int c)	stobUSI(char *, intc)
btosSSI(signed short int n, char *s, int c)	stobSSI(char *, int c)
btosF(float n, char *s, int c)	stobF(char *, int c)

Table 7.2: Binary $\Longleftrightarrow$ Character Conversion Functions

and the receiver to sort out. If you are sending integer or floating point data etc. it will be necessary to re-interpret the data correctly.

There are some functions available for converting various 'C' variable types to a character format and vice versa within the *simplmisc* library. These functions are shown in Table 7.2. The *btos* functions are of type void and the *stob* functions return the number type desired. The *int c* appearing in each function is the width of type *int* on the host in question. For example, on a 32-bit system the int width is 4.

7.6 Summary

In this chapter we covered a great deal of material. The most important points to remember are:

- Surrogates are programs that occur in sender/receiver pairs and communicate with each other remotely via some communication protocol.

- Networked SIMPL is accomplished by the use of surrogate pairs.

- Surrogate pairs currently utilize either TCP/IP or RS-232 communication protocols.

- Required programs to enable the use of surrogates are the protocolRouter, surrogateTcp for TCP/IP, and surrogateRS232 as well as rs232_rw for RS-232.

- There are some specialized surrogates also available for Tcl and for QNX.

7.7   Next Chapter

In the next chapter we are going to begin discussing the importance of testable code as good programming practice and how this concept is furthered and made easier by the use of SIMPL.

Part III

SIMPL Toolkit

Chapter 8

Testing Framework

Almost all real world problems that the SIMPL toolkit would be used to solve are complex. We saw in Chapter 3 on sofwareICs that SIMPL promotes the decomposition of complex problems into islands of manageable complexity. We also saw in Chapter 5 that those SIMPL modules are readily extendable. None of this would matter much if the SIMPL modules and the SIMPL application were not readily testable.

Author Kent Beck's book[1] on the Extreme Programming development approach expounds at length on the importance of testable code in improving project success metrics. In the ideal Extreme Programming project environment the culture is such that tests are created before the code is written. While this ideal is difficult to maintain in practice, we are going to show that the SIMPL testing framework (STF) promotes good coding practices.

- Testable code is an integral part of any successful software development methodology.

- Testable code requires the ability to stimulate all the execution paths without disturbing the executables to do the stimulation.

- Testable code is greatly facilitated if the toolkit under which the application was developed allows for complexity encapsulation, preferably as independent modules.

- Testable code is easier if the test tools can be written in the best language for the task rather than just the language of the application.

---

[1]Extreme Programming Explained by Kent Beck, Addison-Wesley Pub., 2000, ISBN 0-201-61641-6

- If the application being tested is going to be deployed across a network, testable code dictates that unit tests can be run without the network.

- Testable code is enhanced if the execution sequences are always deterministic and predictable. More importantly, this determinism persists even if any particular section of the application comes under load.

- If the developer can extend functionality in the application with a low probability of affecting existing functionality, testability increases.

Before moving on allow us to digress. Much is written and said about the need to document code. We encounter this often in our consulting practice. One of the stated purposes of good documentation is to reduce the learning curve for a new developer charged with the repair or extension of a software application once the original development team has been disbanded. While documentation is important, we believe that it is overrated as a cost effective means to reduce such learning curves. The production and maintenance of a good testing framework is a much more cost effective way to jump start the second team developer. Furthermore, the deployment of an effective testing framework will also lower the costs associated with feature delivery in the original developer team. Like documentation however, unless the original team embraces the concept of a testing framework from the outset, it will be diminished in effectiveness. Alas, retrofitting a good testing framework after the fact is as difficult to achieve as retrofitted documentation.

In this chapter we are going to show how the SIMPL toolkit makes testable code easier. While we are at it, we are going to illustrate the SIMPL design methodology.

In many programming shops, testing (or QA) is viewed as a separate activity from code design and programming. To make matters worse, this separation of responsibility often leads to separate toolsets for programmers and for testers. This separation is unfortunate because testable code needs to be designed into the project from the outset. By definition the software developer needs to be intimately involved.

Software developers hate testing.

This presents a challenge; how do you get developers to adopt a testable code approach?

You have to keep things simple and you have to:

1. Make the testing framework out of the same toolkit primitives used by the developer (eg. text files, scripts, symbolic links etc.).

2. Demonstrate convincingly that the added effort required to build and maintain this testing framework is more than offset by the reduction in time to market for mainline code.

The SIMPL project knows this all too well. Many of the SIMPL testing framework (STF) ideas co-evolved with the SIMPL codebase itself. As a result we've had to migrate developer test scripts over to the new framework after the fact and this is far from complete. Having said this, the STF has been battle tested on a number of SIMPL projects that we have been involved with. When properly deployed it works.

Tests are usually a painful exercise for developers. SIMPL developers are no exception. Unless you make the toolset quite simple and yet powerful they will tend to avoid this exercise. To promote its use, any testing framework must be accessable from the same environment that the developer is using to create code. A successful testing framework must also be written in a language that the developer is already using or can readily master. Despite the best of intentions, all testing frameworks by definition will need to be customized and extended to meet specific needs. Finally, the project culture needs to promote the creation of the *test tools first* before a line of code is created. SIMPL can't address the project culture but the STF can facilitate such a culture when it does exist.

The STF thinks of all software tests as being decomposable into three distinct stages:

1. The setup of environment, database tables, configuration files and so on.

2. The actual execution of the test.

3. The examination of the results.

The STF maps these three steps onto three scripts organized in a simple file tree under the environment variable TEST_HOME (see Figure 8.1).

While in simpler projects one could reasonably manage such a file tree by hand, it rapidly becomes tedious on large real world projects. Tedium is a disincentive for promoting the testing framework's uptake into the project culture.

As such the STF has evolved a series of PATH located wrapper scripts which can be executed from any location in the developer tree. In Figure 8.1 we see three of these wrapper scripts illustrated for a fictional test 1234.

$TEST_HOME/testing/test1234/

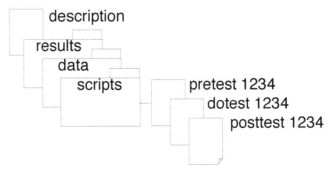

Figure 8.1: SIMPL Test Framework

Let us illustrate the STF by way of a progressively more complex example. The SIMPL project maintains the elements of the SIMPL testing framework as a separate tarball. The installation is described on the project website and also in Appendix A. Once installed the STF should have populated the SIMPL_HOME/scripts area with a series of wrapper scripts with names like seetest, pretest, posttest, copytest etc. If you take a look at those wrapper scripts you will find three scripts which align themselves very well to these three stages described previously:

1. pretest - The setup of the testing environment.

2. dotest - The actual execution of the test.

3. posttest - The examination of the results.

The degree to which each of these scripts is used depends on the project itself. In simpler projects the configuration is all self contained within the dotest script. Similarly, the examination (posttest) stage often consists of a simple observation of behaviour. Nonetheless, it is good practice to maintain and run all three scripts for each test. Experienced STF testers take advantage to make each of these scripts quite verbose in order to document the test in question more fully.

Testing, like software development, is one part creativity and five parts organization. To help with the organization part the STF is going to allow our tests to be identified by a freeform string. Most users will use a numbering scheme to classify their tests but this is not a necessary requirement for these scripts.

Another useful thing to know about the STF wrapper scripts are that they have built in *usage* which can be accessed by simply typing the STF wrapper script name without any arguments; eg. **seetest**.

There are two ways to create a new STF test. You can cause the STF to dip into its templates to create the new test files or you can copy an existing test case. Since we are starting afresh, we haven't got any tests yet to copy so we will start by invoking the templates. Type:

seetest 0001

What should have happened is that a new subdirectory called **test0001** should have been created at **$TEST_HOME/testing**.

Inside that subdirectory a file called **description** should appear. The contents of that are straight text and will reflect the template at this stage. Inside a further subdirectory called **scripts** a set of templated scripts called **setup, runtest, and whathappened** should appear.

NOTE: In what follows we use the scripts *seetest, pretest, dotest, and posttest* to edit the the files *description, setup, runtest, and whathappened* respectively. The scripts seetest, pretest, etc. invoke the **vi** editor in order to modify the description, setup, etc. files. If you are not comfortable with *vi* or it is not available on your system, you may edit these files directly with the text editor of your choice.

The first task with a new test is usually to edit the test description file to describe the test case. Type:

seetest 0001 e

This should bring the description file up in the **vi** editor. The STF index (**seetest i**) uses the first two lines in this description file. The second line of the description file is displayed in the index so it should contain a useful summary line. The rest of the description file is free form text which can be used to document the test case covered by this test.

Not all tests will require all three stages that the STF uses. It is good practice however, to maintain each of these three scripts in any case. At a minimum the TEST_NO and TEST_DESC should be edited in each of these three scripts by typing:

pretest 0001 e
dotest 0001 e
posttest 0001 e

and making those changes to reflect the new test. You can verify that each stage can execute by typing the above commands without the "e" for edit command line argument.

We now need something concrete to add to our test. In Chapter 6 we discussed the stimulator softwareIC. This is probably one of the most frequently used (and cloned) SIMPL softwareICs because it is so useful as a sender test stub. Initially we'll focus our attention on the stage two STF script. Using the following,

dotest 0001 e

to edit something like:

```
#!/bin/bash

TEST_NO=0001
TEST_DESC="SIMPL book test 1"

TEST_DIR=$TEST_HOME/testing/test$TEST_NO
OUTFILE=$TEST_DIR/results/test.out

echo "Starting up test #$TEST_NO" | tee $OUTFILE
echo $TEST_DESC | tee -a $OUTFILE
date | tee -a $OUTFILE

cd $SIMPL_HOME/bin
fclogger -n LOGGER > $TEST_DIR/results/junk &

cd $SIMPL_HOME/softwareICs/stimulator/bin
receiver -n BOBR -l LOGGER &

stimulator -n BOBS -r BOBR -l LOGGER -b &

recvTester -n BOBT -s BOBS -f test_001 -l LOGGER

echo stopping stimulator unit test
$SIMPL_HOME/bin/fcslay BOBS
$SIMPL_HOME/bin/fcslay BOBR
$SIMPL_HOME/bin/fcslay LOGGER

echo "Test finished you can run posttest $TEST_NO for result"
```

As part of the stimulator SIMPL softwareIC package there is a task called **recvTester**. If you were to consult the readme file at

$SIMPL_HOME/softwareICs/stimulator/test/readme

you will find an explanation of how to run this recvTester in a manual (two console) mode.

We could integrate this into our testing framework but the two consoles will be difficult to work with. It would be better if we could combine the processes into a single console and run them all in our single runtest script.

The problem is going to be the stimulator itself. In the mode we have been running this code so far it is displaying prompts and expecting keyboard interaction. This kind of activity is all well and good if that process is run in the foreground. If however, you were to try and put the stimulator up in the background you would find it rapidly falling into an infinite loop and running amok. The reasons are complex but in simplest terms it has to do with the ill-defined STDIN file descriptor for a background process and its effect on the select() multiplexing call. The solution is very simple: prevent your background process from writing to STDOUT and your select() on STDIN will remain safely dormant.

Fortunately, our stimulator example contains a command line parameter **-b** to suppress the prompts to STDOUT and rendering it safe to be run in the background. By using this -b command line option, we can combine up those two consoles described in the stimulator readme into a single script that we illustrated above.

Go ahead and run the first two steps of your test by typing:

pretest 0001
dotest 0001

At the prompt in the dotest script simply type

-> q

to quit and shutdown the test.

Before we go any further it is important to understand what just happened in this test. From that readme once again we see that recvTester is getting its *instructions* from a very simple flat file called:

$SIMPL_HOME/softwareICs/data/test_001

This file currently looks like:

```
#=========================================
# demo of automated stimulator testing
#=========================================
# Test 001
#
Test hi
Sleep 2
Test hello
```

The recvTester contains a crude parser which can:

- Discard lines which are blank.

- Discard lines which begin with #.

- Interpret all other lines as two flavours:

  - Those that begin with the letter "T" - Test
  - Those that begin with the letter "S" - Sleep

The *Sleep* line is taken as a command to do just that: put recvTester to sleep for the number of seconds specified as the second field on the line.

The *Test* line is taken to mean "**Compose and send a TEST_MSG using the second parameter as the string**".

In other words our little test here involved sending two messages:

hi
hello

to our stimulator via its SIMPL interface. The stimulator in turn would dutifully send those on to our **receiver** the actual object of our test.

If we were to examine our trace log,

$TEST_HOME/testing/test0001/results/junk

it might look something like:

```
fclogger starting
[receiver:initialize ] 074015.205 myName=<BOBR> myslot=0
[receiver:initialize ] 074015.207 trace logger mask = 0x00FF
[receiver:receiver   ] 074015.208 starting
```

```
[stimulat:initialize ] 074015.220 myName=<BOBS> myslot=0
[stimulat:initialize ] 074015.221 trace logger mask = 0x00FF
[recvTest:initialize ] 074015. myName=<BOBT> myslot=0
[recvTest:initialize ] 074015.236 stim name=<BOBS> stimslot=3
[recvTest:initialize ] 074015.236 full infile=<~/softwareICs/data/test_001>
[recvTest:initialize ] 074015.237 trace logger mask = 0x00FF
[recvTest:recvTester ] 074015.237 starting
[recvTest:runtest    ] 074015.238 filename=<~/softwareICs/data/test_001>
[stimulat:stimulator ] 074015.260 TEST str=<hi>
[receiver:receiver   ] 074015.262 TEST str=<hi>
[receiver:receiver   ] 074015.262 TEST reply str=<reply #0>
[stimulat:hndlReply  ] 074015.263 TEST reply str=<reply #0>
[stimulat:stimulator ] 074017.275 TEST str=<hello>
[receiver:receiver   ] 074017.276 TEST str=<hello>
[receiver:receiver   ] 074017.277 TEST reply str=<reply #1>
[stimulat:hndlReply  ] 074017.277 TEST reply str=<reply #1>
[recvTest:runtest    ] 074017.279 rc=-1
[recvTest:recvTester ] 074026.857 done
```

Notice the **receiver** lines with the **TEST** message displayed. These are the key lines we want to see in our log if our test was successful. Note that if we were to run this junk file through a series of *greps* we could extract just these lines:

cat junk | grep receiver | grep "TEST str"

If you were to do this you should end up with:

```
[receiver:receiver   ] 074015.262 TEST str=<hi>
[receiver:receiver   ] 074017.276 TEST str=<hello>
```

If we were to arrange to redirect this *grep* output to a file, we could then prepare an expected result file. A simple *diff* between these two files would give us a pass/fail criterion for this test. To accomplish this we have to deal with the trace logger date stamps in our output because these will presumably change each time we run our test and ruin our *diff* strategy.

We can massage our output file through a set of filters to accomplish what we want. If we examine our trace log extract above carefully, we can decide what we want our little filter to do with an incoming line prior to printing it to stdout. The first thing to notice is that the time stamp section is all lined up on a nice fixed column on every line.

If we could simply replace the digits in this time stamp with a fixed pattern, we could be on our way to using **diff** as our pass/fail criterion. If you count columns you will find that the time stamp is between column 25 and 34. Therefore we need a filter which when run as:

cat junk | funfilter

will simply replace the time stamp field (ie. col 25-34) with **xxxxxx.xxx** Here's a version for such a filter:

```
/*=======================================
*
* funfilter.c
*
* Main source file for
* SIMPL book test filter
*
*=====================================*/

#include <stdio.h>

int main()
{
char line[80];

while(fgets(line, 79, stdin) != NULL)
  {
  if(strlen(line) > 28)
    {
    line[24]='x';
    line[25]='x';
    line[26]='x';
    line[27]='x';
    line[28]='x';
    line[29]='x';
    line[31]='x';
    line[32]='x';
    line[33]='x';
    }
  printf("%s",line);
  }
}
```

Go ahead and run your junk file through your newly minted funfilter and you should see the time stamp get replaced by x's. We now have all the tools to do that pass/fail part within our posttest script. Once again, for those of you familiar with the **vi** editor you can simply type:

posttest 0001 e

What we will need to integrate into this script are the following "stages".

- The grep sequence above to isolate the lines we really want from the trace log.

- The funfilter sequence above to replace the time stamp with x's.

- A diff comparison to see if these lines match our expected ones.

Here's a posttest script which will generate a pass/fail notification by comparing with a hand crafted expected output file at:

$TEST_HOME/testing/test0001/data/grepfile.001

```
#!/bin/bash

TEST_NO=0001
TEST_DESC="SIMPL book test1"

TEST_DIR=$TEST_HOME/testing/test$TEST_NO
OUTFILE=$TEST_DIR/results/aftershot

MYFILTER=$HOME/simplbook/src/funfilter
GREPFILE=$TEST_DIR/results/grepfile
GOODFILE=$TEST_DIR/data/grepfile.001

echo "preparing results - test#$TEST_NO, please wait" | tee $OUTFILE
date | tee -a $OUTFILE

echo "=======================" | tee -a $OUTFILE
cat $TEST_DIR/results/test.out | tee -a $OUTFILE

echo "=======================" | tee -a $OUTFILE
echo "Here is the test output" | tee -a $OUTFILE

cat $TEST_DIR/results/junk \
 | grep receiver \
 | grep "TEST str"\
 | $MYFILTER | tee -a $OUTFILE | tee $GREPFILE

echo "=======================" | tee -a $OUTFILE

echo "comparing with expected results" | tee -a $OUTFILE
diff $GREPFILE $GOODFILE
DONE=$?
if [ $DONE = 0 ]
```

```
then
 echo "*** PASSED ***"  | tee −a $OUTFILE
else
 echo "*** FAILED ***"  | tee −a $OUTFILE
fi

echo "=======================" | tee −a $OUTFILE

echo "done preparing results for test#$TEST_NO"
```

There are more examples of the SIMPL Testing Framework in both the SIMPL project tarball and the project part of this book beginning with Chapter 10.

8.1   Summary

We have gone into to some detail in this section to illustrate the SIMPL Testing Framework (STF). We have shown how a test can be built up from basics using the public softwareICs code repository for seed code. Using the SIMPL trace logger output we have shown how with a few simple steps one can make the STF yield a pass/fail criterion.

Testability is an essential ingredient of any software application. The STF makes managing the testable SIMPL applications easier.

8.2   Next Chapter

In the next chapter we are going to take a look at a little known feature inherent in the SIMPL design: virtualization through multiple sandboxes.

Chapter 9

SIMPL Sandbox

In the previous chapter we talked about the SIMPL Testing Framework (STF). Testable code is an important feature of SIMPL applications. One of the under-used features SIMPL is the ability to run duplicate or parallel applications in separate SIMPL sandboxes. This can help with SIMPL testability.

There are many scenarios where multiple SIMPL sandboxes might find uses. One of the obvious candidates would be to facilitate release management of a multiple SIMPL module application. When a new version of that application becomes available, it might be prudent to deploy it first in a separate SIMPL sandbox while maintaining the original deployment in the original SIMPL sandbox. That way, if issues arose that called for a temporary rollback this could easily be accommodated.

Recall from Chapter 4 on the SIMPL core library, that SIMPL **name_locate** calls work off a special directory denoted by the FIFO_PATH environment variable. We call that directory the *SIMPL sandbox*. Most SIMPL developers employ only one single SIMPL sandbox and export only one global FIFO_PATH variable. However, environment variables can be easily overridden in a start up script where they only have local scope. In the examples below the SIMPL benchmark is run in two different sandboxes with the same SIMPL name in each case.

```
#!/bin/bash
# startup for sandbox 1

export FIFO_PATH=/home/sandbox1

cd $SIMPL_HOME/benchmarks/bin
receiver -n BOBR &
```

```
#!/bin/bash
# startup for sandbox 2

export FIFO_PATH=/home/sandbox2

cd $SIMPL_HOME/benchmarks/bin
receiver -n BOBR &
```

Multiple sandboxes which are set in startup (or STF scripts) can be viewed with the same lens as the much more complex virtual machines.

The reasons for doing something like this are not unlike the reasons why someone might want to run multiple OS images in virtual machines. Principal amongst those reasons is that this mode of operation can offer flexibility on start up and shutdown of one SIMPL application without affecting the status of the others. Another reason people use virtualization is to facilitate migration to (and testing of) newer versions of the same application. Multiple SIMPL sandboxes can help in that regard also. Another characteristic of virtualization is that multiple virtual environments almost always exist on a single physical machine. This is certainly the case for multiple SIMPL sandboxes.

Virtualization is normally used to provide an isolated working environment. This is particularly true for the namespace. ie. different SIMPL sandboxes can reuse the same SIMPL names. However, occasionally it is desirable to pass a SIMPL message between a SIMPL process in one sandbox to another SIMPL process in another sandbox. An example may be when a SIMPL application undergoes a significant upgrade in business logic but not in a GUI interface. The original application including the GUI could be left running in one sandbox and the new business logic modules in a second sandbox. In order to *share* the GUI module the new business logic would need to exchange inter-sandbox messages. For this purpose tunnels are used for inter-sandbox transport in a manner not dissimilar to surrogates for network messaging.

As you may recall from Chapter 4, SIMPL exchanges messages in shared memory and synchronizes this exchange by passing the shared memory ID over a FIFO.

A tunnel is a SIMPL process that SIMPL name attaches as its counterpart in the other sandbox and connects two FIFOs together. Tunnels come in two flavours:

- Tunnels for the send exchange between the sender and the receiver.

- Tunnels for the reply exchange back to the sender.

A typical sandbox with tunnels might look like Figure 9.1.

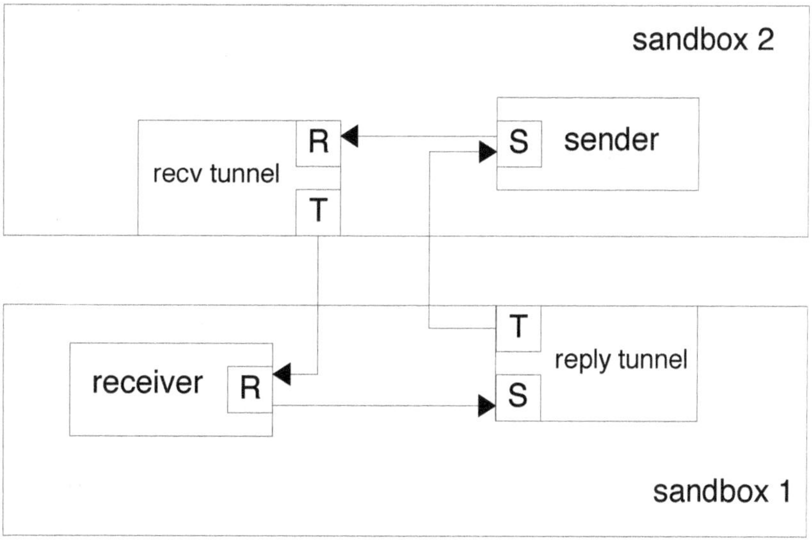

Figure 9.1: SIMPL Sandbox

We want to keep our sender and receiver code completely agnostic to the presence of multiple sandboxes and tunnels between those sandboxes. This is much the same viewpoint which was adopted to make SIMPL processes network agnostic through the use of surrogates. As such, a tunnel is really just a surrogate for inter-sandbox communication.

In fact all a tunnel has to do is to reroute the shared memory ID from one FIFO to another (the **T** box in Figure 9.1). Since the actual SIMPL message is stored in a shared memory area owned by the sender, and we are restricting tunnels to sandboxes on the same machine, the rest of the SIMPL message exchange can go as before.

Let's examine the sender->receiver message exchange illustrated in Figure 9.1. As already mentioned, the sender and the receiver are straightforward SIMPL applications with nothing special added for inter-sandbox message exchange.

The receiver tunnel process is activated on sandbox 1 to act as the *placeholder* for the actual receiver which lives in sandbox 2. In fact, this tunnel assumes the SIMPL name of the real receiver. As such, when the sender does the ***name_locate*** to begin the message exchange it finds what it believes to be the desired receiver local to its own sandbox. The SIMPL message exchange begins with the sender in sandbox 1 adding the bytes associated with the message into its own block of shared memory. Next, the sender pushes the shared memory ID for this message block onto the FIFO which connects the sender with what it believes to be the receiver, but what is actually the receiver tunnel process.

Meanwhile, when the receiver tunnel is activated it establishes a second connection to the receive FIFO associated with its real receiver in sandbox 2. When the shared memory ID arrives in the receiver tunnel's SIMPL FIFO it is simply copied over to this sandbox 2 FIFO and the receiver tunnel's job is done. The real receiver now sees the shared memory ID arrive in its FIFO and reacts as if a normal SIMPL message has arrived. ie. opens the shared memory segment and accesses the data.

Now, a second tunnel process was started along with the SIMPL receiver in sandbox 2: the reply tunnel. This reply tunnel assumes the SIMPL name of the sender in the sandbox 1 and upon start up opens a second channel back to the sender's reply FIFO.

Once the receiver processes the message it adds the response data back into the shared memory segment and pushes a return code onto the sender's reply FIFO which it believes is the reply tunnel process (because it has the same SIMPL name as the sender). Once the reply tunnel process sees this return code it simply copies it over to the real reply FIFO and its job is complete.

The sender then sees the response as if it came from the receiver. We have achieved our objective of a totally transparent SIMPL message pass between two SIMPL sandboxes.

9.1   Summary

Virtualization has become popular because it is useful. Virtualization of SIMPL via multiple SIMPL sandboxes will become popular because it too is useful.

9.2   Next Chapter

In the next section we are going to explore a fictitious SIMPL project with the aim of illustrating the SIMPL approach to application building in a more concrete manner.

Part IV

SIMPL Example Project

Chapter 10

A SIMPL Project - Putting It All Together

The aim of this part of the book is to explore a straightforward example project. After all, most of our readers will also be programmers and will want to see a software tool like SIMPL in action. They will want to see the project source code and even modify it as they explore and read along. As such we want to choose an example project which includes as many aspects of SIMPL as practical yet doesn't take up too much space with unnecessary details. Our project, an Internet distributed collection of word and number puzzle solvers, would not likely be found in the business world. However, we'll use it to illustrate many of the principles discussed in the book so far and perhaps even more importantly we'll show that SIMPL programming can be fun.

10.1   Project Specification

The project we have in mind is admittedly contrived. Hopefully it is complex enough to show as many facets of the SIMPL approach as possible, but not be so complex as to lose the story thread.

The specification (or spec for short) for our collection of word and number puzzle solvers calls for both the solver engines and the puzzle submitting clients to be connected via the Internet. The engines will be hosted on servers. The users will access those puzzle engines from any of the popular desktop OSs.

This is a somewhat daunting spec at first glance. We are going to illustrate how the SIMPL approach involves translating this spec into a SIMPL system picture. Armed with this full system picture we will chose to implement the simplest subsystem first.

10.2   The Design Meeting

Typically the designers, armed with the spec, would convene a meeting where various implementations would be discussed and debated on a white board. The outcome of such a meeting would be a system picture something like Figure 10.1.

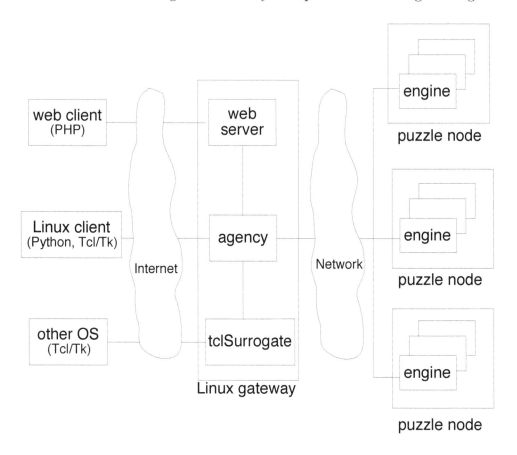

Figure 10.1: System Picture

On the left hand side the various client interfaces are illustrated. On the right hand side the various puzzle solver engines are illustrated. In the middle is the central Linux gateway which connects the two. For Linux desktops it will be possible to submit puzzles using either a Python/Tk or a Tcl/Tk client implementation. For the other desktop OSs such as Windows or Mac, a Tcl/Tk client implementation will be available. All of the desktops will support web applet access via the Tcl/Tk Firefox plug-in as well as a PHP based web interface.

The puzzle solver engine nodes will be restricted to Linux OS servers. The engines themselves could be implemented in any number of programming languages but we'll restrict ourselves to 'C'. 'C' is a great language for implementing SIMPL modules and it is powerful enough for our puzzle solving algorithms. To handle the simultaneous client load the engines would be implemented as forking *agents* (recall Chapter 6).

The gateway node will be configured to host a web server and the SIMPL TCP/IP surrogates as well as the tclSurrogate. In addition, the gateway node will host the central puzzle solver module derived from the agency softwareIC to allow multiple concurrent Sudoku sessions. Recall Section 6.6 in Chapter 6. The Linux clients will use the TCP/IP surrogate pathway to establish SIMPL connectivity with the puzzle engines. The other desktop OS clients and the browser applets will use the tclSurrogate interface to establish SIMPL connectivity. The gateway web server will host the PHP interface into the system.

The system picture has certainly helped solidify our spec, but it's still complex. Next up, the design team needs to come up with a work plan.

10.3   The First Cut

The SIMPL approach closely follows Kent Beck's Extreme Programming[1] when it comes to choosing the initial implementation. We'll pick the simplest possible subsystem which has any business value and implement that first. We'll do this with full confidence that this base system can be evolved in a systematic manner to arrive at the final feature set described in the spec.

This approach has several advantages. Firstly, it gets the team energized and productive in the quickest possible way. Secondly, it gives the users some tangible progress in the form of usable code at the earliest date. This lowers both the ultimate cost and risk associated with any software project. In addition, it provides the project team with the adaptability to adjust to the invariably changing spec.

How do we simplify our system picture to this base implementation? The spec calls for multiple puzzle engines. We'll settle on Sudoku as our first engine implementation. Sudoku has a tidy set of puzzle rules and a straightforward interface so it makes a good candidate. The spec calls for several different client

---

[1]Extreme Programming Explained by Kent Beck, Addison-Wesley Pub., 2000, ISBN 0-201-61641-6

Figure 10.2: Sudoku Subsystem Picture

implementations. We'll settle on Python as the first go. Why Python? We could have chosen to create the GUI using 'C'/X Windows or Tcl/Tk. Python is a popular object oriented scripting language and would likely have a shorter development time than the other choices. The spec calls for the engine to be a forking agent capable of handling multiple simultaneous clients. We don't need this level of sophistication on the first cut, so we'll settle on an engine which is a primitive SIMPL receiver and a GUI which is a primitive SIMPL sender. (see Figure 10.2).

We'll plan to evolve this base implementation through a series of straightforward transformations into our full feature set. For example, the planned transformation sequence for the engine might look like the following:

- Convert to a forking receiver.

- Convert from a forking receiver to a forking agent.

Similarly the initial Python client software could evolve as:

- Port the Python client to a Tcl/Tk Linux client.

- Port the Tcl/Tk Linux client to a tclSurrogate capable client.

- Port the tclSurrogate client to a web applet.

- Develop a PHP interface which duplicates the functionality above.

10.4   Sudoku

So initially we'll be creating programs that solve sudoku puzzles.[2] To start with let's take look at what makes up a sudoku puzzle. For us it will consist of a 9x9

---

[2]If you wish to follow along with some real code in front of you the entire Sudoku project code is available at **http://www.icanprogram.com/simplBook**.

or a 16x16 matrix of numbers. In the first case, the numbers are the decimals 1-9. In the second case the numbers are the hexadecimals 0-F. When the puzzle is given, only some of the numbers in the matrix are non-blank. A solution to the puzzle involves filling in the blanks such that all rows contain all available numbers with no repetition, all columns contain all available numbers with no repetition and all submatrices, 3x3 and 4x4 respectively also contain all available numbers with no repetition. See Figure 10.3 for an example of typical 9x9 puzzle. The submatrices in the figure appear as shaded or not shaded.

Figure 10.3: A Typical 9x9 Sudoku Puzzle

What would be our approach to this task? Our first cut meeting above proposed an initial solution which consists of a Python GUI to display the puzzle and also some way to accept the correct numerical values. As well, we proposed a 'C' program that solves the puzzles based on the given values. The Python GUI will be a SIMPL sender and the Sudoku engine will be a SIMPL receiver. We are going write one GUI program in Python/Tk and one engine program in 'C'. The end user will use this GUI for collecting input data, sending that data to the engine program and then displaying the solution. The engine program will accept a puzzle and contain an algorithm for solving it.

Notice what has happened here. The modular nature of SIMPL has allowed us not only to simplify our problem into a very basic initial implementation; it has also allowed us to chose programming languages appropriate to each portion of that implementation. Once we can agree on the structure of the SIMPL messages which will be exchanged between these two modules, we are in a position to develop them in a parallel fashion. It appears that we have broken up the task functionality in a way that exploits a natural division of labour. Moreover, we will run the GUI and engine programs on one host, thus eliminating the need for any surrogates and removing any possible problems due to networking issues.

10.5   Summary

At this point the project team has an overall picture. It also has a near term work plan, albeit at a much simpler level than the overall picture. We are going to develop a Sudoku puzzle solver first. We are going to create a Python GUI sender which will exchange messages with a Sudoku puzzle engine which is a SIMPL receiver written in 'C'.

10.6   Next Chapter

In the next chapter we are going to show how the project team begins the actual work by setting up the SIMPL Testing Framework (STF) associated with the Sudoku puzzle solver task.

Chapter 11

Test Plan

At this point the project team has white-boarded the project picture. This project picture has then been simplified into the first piece of work: the Sudoku puzzle solver. The next task for the project team will be to design the SIMPL Testing Framework (STF) tests.

As always there will be unit tests designed to exercise particular SIMPL modules in the Sudoku puzzle solver system. There will also be integration tests whose purpose is to exercise the collective system of all the modules. The following is how the test plan might look:

sb000 Sim/Stim test.

sb001 Sudoku engine unit test.

sb002 Python GUI unit test.

sb003 Tcl/Tk GUI unit test.

sb003s Tcl/Tk GUI unit test with tclSurrogate and local host.

sb004 Python + engine integration test.

sb005 Tcl/Tk + engine integration test.

Of these only sb000, sb001, sb002 and sb004 will be worked on first as these are the tests associated with the Python GUI and the Sudoku puzzle engine. Once we are happy that the Python GUI works as per sb002, the team members working on the Tcl/Tk GUI can begin with sb003, sb003s and sb005.

In pictorial form, the test plan looks like the figures below for the Python phase.

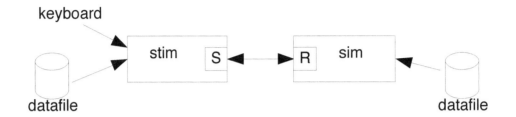

Figure 11.1: sb000 - sim/stim test

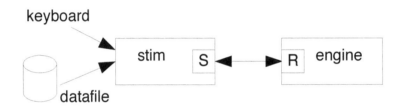

Figure 11.2: sb001 - Sudoku engine unit test

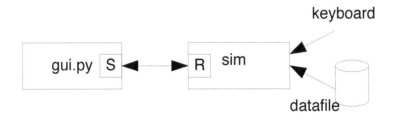

Figure 11.3: sb002 - Python GUI unit test

Figure 11.4: sb004 - Python GUI/Sudoku engine test

The addition of the Tcl/Tk phase results in these tests.

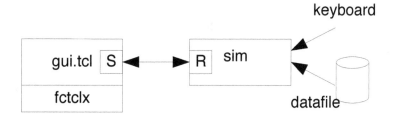

Figure 11.5: sb003 - Tcl GUI unit test

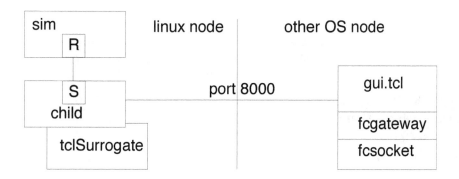

Figure 11.6: sb003s - remote Tcl GUI unit test

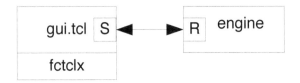

Figure 11.7: sb005 - Tcl GUI/Sudoku engine test

11.1   The Unit Tests

The first five tests are unit tests of the various elements planned for the first phase of work. The Tcl/Tk GUI unit test comes in two flavours because the Tcl/Tk GUI can be run in two distinct modes depending on which library is used to export the SIMPL API:

- The fctclx shared library (sb003).

- The fcgateway Tcl/Tk package (sb003s).

Unit tests are designed to exercise one particular SIMPL module thoroughly. The SIMPL messages originate with, or are absorbed by test stubs in the unit tests, depending on whether the SIMPL module is a receiver or a sender. The purpose for a unit test is to exercise as many pathways through the coded algorithm of the test subject as possible. Take the engine unit test (sb001) for example. We'd want at a minimum to submit a valid, invalid and unsolvable puzzle to test the engine's ability to handle those cases. We'd pay particular attention to the message content being submitted and the message content being replied back. In some projects it may pay to invest the time to automate these unit tests to allow them to be run regularly from a *cron* script and to have them yield a pass/fail criterion. Our example project is simple enough that we'll stick with straightforward hand-run and hand-examined unit tests.

11.2   The Integration Tests

Integration tests on the other hand, are designed to exercise combinations of SIMPL modules which form the full SIMPL application. Integration tests don't often employ test stubs except perhaps at the boundaries where they substitute for real world I/O. In our little example project the two integration tests will not employ any test stubs. The integration tests are employed to test the ability of the entire SIMPL application to work correctly together. This is where one would look for timing issues or GUI usability issues under simulated real world loads.

11.3 Summary

The project team now has a near term test plan. All the tests have been identified and *white-boarded.*

11.4 Next Chapter

In the next chapter we are going to show how the project team begins the actual work by setting up the project directory tree and begins to populate it with seed code that can allow immediate execution of the STF test plan scripts.

Chapter 12

Directory Tree

At this point in the project, we have designed our unit and integration tests for the *simplest possible subimplementation* of our puzzle solver system.

The next step involves making housekeeping decisions on the source code and testing directory tree. Once the tree is designed it will be populated with suitable seed code from the softwareICs (or another suitable) SIMPL code repository.

In our specific case we have settled on a simplified sender-receiver pair for the Sudoku puzzle solver portion of our system. We have designed four unit tests for the various configurations of this pair plus an additional proof test for the stim and sim test stubs themselves.

We have elected to name our project **simplBook**. This will become the apex directory in our tree. To aid in location of this tree on different virtual developer trees, we will designate an environment variable which points to the apex directory. We will call this environment variable: *SIMPLBOOK_HOME*.

Inside this SIMPLBOOK_HOME directory we will create our top level Makefile for the project. When executed, this top level Makefile will build everything associated with the puzzle solver project. A good example of such a top level Makefile is the one associated with the SIMPL toolkit itself. Also residing in this apex directory will be the module subdirectories. In our case we will begin with a subdirectory called *sudoku*. The top level include subdirectory will exist at this level as well. It will be populated with any global headers required by all the modules in the project. Another directory at this level will be called *testing*. This will be home to all the test scripts and data files associated with the SIMPL testing framework described in Chapter 8. Finally, there will be a *bin* directory where all submodule executables will be promoted on a successful *make install*.

At this point our directory tree looks like:


```
/simplBook/Makefile
/simplBook/include/
/simplBook/bin/
/simplBook/sudoku/
/simplBook/testing/
```


The sudoku subdirectory itself will contain a Makefile. This Makefile will be called from the top level Makefile and will be responsible for building all the elements of the sudoku module. Also residing at this level in the tree will be three subdirectories associated with the source code of the sudoku module: *src, include, test*. The src subdirectory will contain the sudoku engine and client source code and the include subdirectory will contain any local header files associated with the sudoku module. The test subdirectory will be home to all the sudoku test stubs. Finally, there will be an intermediate build area for executables associated with the sudoku module in a directory called *bin*. A simple make at the sudoku level will populate this bin subdirectory. Unit test scripts would point into this bin directory for the executables to run.

At this point the sudoku subtree would look like:


```
/simplBook/sudoku/Makefile
/simplBook/sudoku/bin/
/simplBook/sudoku/src/
/simplBook/sudoku/include/
/simplBook/sudoku/test/
```


12.1   Seeding the Code

At this stage we have only populated our tree with a couple of very generic high level Makefiles. It is time to seed the tree with some source code and source code Makefiles so that we can begin the construction of operational test scripts in our framework.

A good place to go for seed code is our softwareICs code repository. Since our unit test design calls for a stimulator a great place to start might be with the stimulator softwareIC source code.[1] We'll need to rearrange things a little because our sudoku/src is going to contain the sudoku engine, a SIMPL receiver. We'll want to move a copy of the receiver.c and receiverInit.c into the sudoku/src directory and rename those as engine. We'll want to move the stimulator code into the sudoku/test subdirectory and rearrange the Makefiles to allow this seed code to compile. The copy of receiver left in the test subdirectory is destined to become the simulator in our unit tests.

At this stage our **sudoku/src** portion of the tree looks something like:

```
/Makefile
/engine.c (copy of receiver.c)
/engineInit.c (copy of receiverInit.c)
```

and **sudoku/test** looks something like:

```
/Makefile
/stimulator.c
/stimulatorInit.c
/stimulatorUtils.c
/sim.c (copied from receiver.c and renamed sim.c)
/simInit.c (copied from receiverInit.c and renamed simInit.c)
```

12.2   Seeding the Tests

If we examine each of these tests we quickly observe that they all are very similar to the SIMPL unit test for softwareICs stimulator (s0008). As such we can use the *copytest* wrapper script[2] to clone that SIMPL test six times into each of our tests.

copytest s0008 sb000

With a quick edit for each description and each test script suite to insert the actual test number in place of the SIMPL test number we have six operational

---

[1] If you wish to follow along with some code in front of you, we have included a representative body of seed code in the main simplBook sudoku tarball under the **sudoku.seed** subdirectory. The process of obtaining and installing that tarball is described at **http://www.icanprogram.com/simplBook**.

[2] The SIMPL Testing Framework will install a number of wrapper scripts under SIMPL_HOME/scripts, of which copytest is one.

tests. They don't do what we want as yet, but that is the subject of the next chapter.

Once we get the whole show recompiling we will want to change the runtest script associated with test sb000 (the sim-stim test) to pickup its executables from our new build area. At this point test sb000 can be run, albeit with the same result as when it ran as a SIMPL unit test clone.

12.3   Summary

In this chapter we have designed our entire directory tree for the first phase of this project. We have populated that tree with seed code from the SIMPL softwareICs repository and the SIMPL STF tests. After renaming some files and rearranging some Makefiles we can get the whole thing compiling and our main unit test can be executed.

12.4   Next Chapter

We are now ready to begin the actual Sudoku design process. In the next chapter we are going to begin by designing the tokenized messages we are going to require for our Sudoku puzzle solver and we are going to begin to show how the header files for our project will be renamed and populated with our new message structures.

Chapter 13

Sims and Stims

"A 'C' programmer only writes one program, then beats it up for evermore."
–Anonymous

At this point we have various unit tests defined. We have populated these unit tests with seed code from the SIMPL softwareICs repository. Everything compiles and executes, only it doesn't contain any Sudoku code as yet.

We have talked previously about the extendability of SIMPL. This is usually taken to infer that SIMPL designs readily allow simpler things to be transformed into more complex forms. In the real world of programming this is often true but it is not always the case. It is also possible to take more complicated systems and rework them into simpler systems because they were originally designed with SIMPL in mind. In this section we are going to do just that, take the relevant softwareICs as a starting point and simplify them into the sort of code that we need to fulfill our teaching obligations to the reader and obtain code snips that are amenable to the book. We should mention that SIMPL designs also provide convenient lateral modifications. ie. from one system to another of similar complexity. This would be the case when an existent system has the sort of design and message passing requirements needed for a proposed system: Why reinvent the wheel?

Now that we have seed code compiling, our method for migrating this code to the final form will be essentially iterative following these steps:

Step 1: Make changes to seed code.

Step 2: Get the code recompiling.

Step 3: Run the unit test to see results in trace log.

Step 4: Go back to Step 1.

The advantage of starting with a fully trace log enabled body of seed code and an operational unit test cannot be overstated. This allows the Sudoku developer team to make methodical and incremental changes to the code all the while ensuring that it recompiles and executes at each stage. Problems are quickly discovered and easily isolated and repaired using this approach to program development.

13.1   What sort of Messages Do We Need?

Our seed code contains tokenized SIMPL messages which are exchanged between the stimulator and the engine (or sim). However, at this stage these tokenized message definitions are still those from the seed code in the repository. The Sudoku developer team will now need to begin the SIMPL code design process by defining the tokens and message structures that will be required to operate the Sudoku puzzle engine.

The first message that we need to define pertains to the information gathered by the GUI and then sent to the engine for processing. The available information is:

1. The size of puzzle to be solved, 9x9 or 16x16.

2. The values of the given matrix elements. That is 1-9 or 0-F and a blank for an unknown value.

The size of the puzzle could be relayed by the message token. The body of the message could be either 9x9=81 or 16x16=256 characters with the given matrix elements set to the appropriate numbers and the unknown values set to spaces. This is all the information that the engine program requires in order to attempt a solution.

The second message that we need to define is the reply message to the GUI from the engine. What does the GUI require? It simply needs to know whether the puzzle could be solved and if so, what the solution is. Again, we could use the token value of the message to indicate success or failure. The body of the message could be the solution.

From a 'C' code perspective, the sent and reply messages would both look like the following:

engineMsgs.h

```
typedef enum
  {
  DO_9,
  DO_16,
  PUZZLE_FAILURE,
  ERROR,
  BAD_TOKEN,
  MAX_ENGINE_TOKENS
  } ENGINE_TOKEN;

typedef struct
  {
  int token;
  char elements[256]; // maximum possible size
  } SUDOKU_MSG;
```

We have defined a message structure of type SUDOKU_MSG. The GUI can set the structure member called token to define the puzzle size and the structure member character array called elements can take up to the largest size of puzzle. The engine can use the same structure by setting the token to:

1. DO_9/DO_16 in the case of a successful solution.

2. PUZZLE_FAILURE in the case of no solution.

3. ERROR if a problem of some sort is encountered.

4. BAD_TOKEN if the received token is unknown.

The engine will return the solution in the elements array in the case of a successful solution. Note that this situation is somewhat unusual in that the structures of the sent and replied messages are usually very different. Nevertheless, the simplicity of the situation is gratifying. We have now defined the interaction between the GUI and the engine.

Now that we have the tokenized messages designed it is time to add that to our main Sudoku engine header file. In our case that header is now called *receiverMsgs.h*. We will begin by changing the name to *engineMsgs.h* and proceed to add our tokens and tokenized message structures to that file. We'll have

to change all occurrences of receiverMsgs.h in our seed code to engineMsgs.h to
get things safely recompiling once again. Recall that receiverMsgs.h is a general
type of header file like the softwareICs that we are making specific to our task.

13.2   Global Variables

The global variables we will be specifying in our engine and simulator currently
share a common header called *receiver.h*. We need to rectify that now by cloning
that header once and renaming the pair as *engine.h* and *sim.h*. The same is true
of the header containing function prototypes: *receiverProto.h* which gets cloned
as *engineProto.h* and *simProto.h*. Once again all instances of these previous
header names are simply replaced by the new ones and all of the code should
recompile and run once again.

Each of the SIMPL modules (stimulator, engine and simulator) are composed
of multiple source files. We have adopted the **_ALLOC** scheme for sorting
out whether those global variables are declared outright (as in the source file
containing main()) or as **extern** (as in Init and Utils files).

13.3   Simulator and Stimulator

At this point we still have identical seed code for both our simulator and our
engine. It makes sense at this stage to focus on the simulator recognizing that
once we get that operational, the engine can absorb those changes and evolve
from there. Furthermore, our simulator can then be added to the GUI unit
tests (sb002, sb003, and sb003s, see Figures 11.3, 11.5, and 11.6) as the engine
substitute.

Recall that a simulator is a stub program whose only purpose is to receive
a canned message from a sender and then reply to that sender in order to aid
in testing the SIMPL aspect of the sender code, ie. the messaging scheme. It
processes as little as possible because its main purpose is to exercise the SIMPL
interface. In this way a sender program can be developed independently of a
receiver program. For our example, we won't need the engine in order to receive
a message from the GUI. The sim program will simply consist of a program that
receives and replies a canned message of type SUDOKU_MSG. We will write the
sim in 'C' so that we can use the structure definition as it stands. As well, when
we are satisfied with the efficacy of the sim we can use it as a solid starting point
for the engine. The essential difference between sim and engine will be that the
later contains the complete Sudoku processing algorithm.

We also want to develop a stub for the GUI program. Fortunately, we have inherited a very capable stimulator when we seeded our code from the SIMPL repository. Recall that a stimulator is a small program that sends a canned message to a receiver and then obtains a canned reply from that receiver. In this way a receiver program can be developed and tested independently of any sender program. For our example, the stimulator program will simply consist of a program that sends a canned message of type SUDOKU_MSG to the engine and then obtains a reply either indicating failure or success and a solution. The stimulator seed code is written in 'C' whereas our first GUI will be written in Python. Nevertheless, the stimulator will be able to ascertain the veracity of the SIMPL communications to the SIMPL receivers in all of our unit tests. Later we can take the essence of the stimulator and base the actual GUI programs upon this.[1]

13.4 Simulator Logic

As has already been stated, the purpose of the simulator is to act as a SIMPL stub for the receiver we have called the engine. Let's take a look at the code for the sim and examine the salient points. We will start with sim.h and simProto.h, header files containing definitions peculiar to sim. Note that the message and token definitions used by the sim program are the same as defined earlier as SUDOKU_MSG and ENGINE_TOKEN respectively.

sim.h

```
1   // defined macros
2   #define  SIZE_9         9
3   #define  SIZE_16        16
4   #define  SUCCESS        0
5   #define  FAIL           −1
6   #define  MAX_MSG_SIZE    1024
7
8   // for the logger
9   #define  SIM_MARK       0x00000001
10  #define  SIM_FUNC_IO    0x00000002
11  #define  SIM_MISC       0x00000010
12
13  // global variables
14  _ALLOC char datapath[80];
```

---

[1]If you wish to follow along with some real code in front of you the entire Sudoku project code is available at **http://www.icanprogram.com/simplBook**.

```
15  _ALLOC int size; // size of the incoming puzzle (9x9 or 16x16)
16  _ALLOC char array[SIZE_16 * SIZE_16]; // maximum size
17  _ALLOC unsigned int globalMask; // for the logger
18
19  // for the incoming and outgoing messages
20  _ALLOC char inArea[MAX_MSG_SIZE];
21  _ALLOC char outArea[MAX_MSG_SIZE];
```

lines 2-6 Definitions used by sim code.

lines 9-11 Definitions used in trace logger function calls.

lines 14-17 Global variable declarations.

lines 20-21 Global incoming and outgoing message buffer declarations.

simProto.h

```
1  void initialize(int, char **);
2  void myUsage(void);
3  int process(SUDOKU_MSG *, SUDOKU_MSG *);
4  void readData(char *);
```

lines 1-4 Function prototype declarations.

line 1 All program initializations are carried out in this function at startup.

line 2 Program usage in the case of an incorrect command line.

line 3 The function that carries out the actual program processing.

line 4 The function that reads the appropriate data file.

sim.c

```
1  // standard headers
2  #include <stdio.h>
3  #include <stdlib.h>
4  #include <unistd.h>
5  #include <time.h>
6  #include <string.h>
7
8  // sim program headers
```

```
9   #define _ALLOC
10  #include "sim.h"
11  #undef _ALLOC
12  #include "engineMsgs.h"
13  #include "simProto.h"
14
15  // SIMPL headers
16  #include "simpl.h"
17
18  // for the logger
19  #define _ALLOC
20  #include "loggerVars.h"
21  #undef _ALLOC
22  #include "loggerProto.h"
23
24  /*=========================================================
25      sim - entry point
26  =========================================================*/
27  int main(int argc, char **argv, char **envp)
28  {
29  char *fn = "sim";
30  int x_it = 0;
31  int nbytes;
32  char *sender;
33  SUDOKU_MSG *in = (SUDOKU_MSG *)inArea;
34  SUDOKU_MSG *out = (SUDOKU_MSG *)outArea;
35  int msgSize;
36  int ret;
37
38  // initialize variables, ready program for SIMPL communications etc.
39  initialize(argc, argv);
40
41  // log the startup
42  fcLogx(__FILE__, fn, globalMask, SIM_MARK, "starting");
43
44  while (!x_it) // loop indefinitely receiving & replying to messages
45     {
46     // receive incoming messages
47     nbytes = Receive(&sender, inArea, MAX_MSG_SIZE);
48     if (nbytes == -1)
49        {
50        fcLogx(__FILE__, fn, SIM_MARK, SIM_MARK,
51          "Receive error-%s", whatsMyError());
52        continue;
53        }
54
```

```
55    // decide course of action based on value of the message token
56    switch (in->token)
57      {
58      // a 9x9 puzzle
59      case DO_9:
60        // set necessary variables
61        size = SIZE_9;
62
63        // try to match the puzzle and compose reply message
64        ret = process(in, out);
65        if (ret != -1)
66          {
67          // success
68          out->token = DO_9;
69          // use msgSize NOT sizeof(MSG), C may pad out structure
70          msgSize = sizeof(int) + size * size * sizeof(char);
71          }
72        else
73          {
74          // failure, no solution
75          out->token = PUZZLE_FAILURE;
76          msgSize = sizeof(int);
77          }
78
79        // reply results to sender
80        if (Reply(sender, out, msgSize) == -1)
81          {
82          fcLogx(__FILE__, fn, SIM_MARK, SIM_MARK,
83            "Reply error-%s", whatsMyError());
84          }
85        break;
86
87      // a 16x16 puzzle
88      case DO_16:
89        // set necessary variables
90        size = SIZE_16;
91
92        // try to match the puzzle and compose reply message
93        ret = process(in, out);
94        if (ret != -1)
95          {
96          // success
97          out->token = DO_16;
98          // use msgSize NOT sizeof(MSG), C may pad out structure
99          msgSize = sizeof(int) + size * size * sizeof(char);
100          }
```

```
101          else
102            {
103            // failure, no solution
104            out->token = PUZZLE_FAILURE;
105            msgSize = sizeof(int);
106            }
107
108          // reply results to sender
109          if (Reply(sender, out, msgSize) == -1)
110            {
111            fcLogx(__FILE__, fn, SIM_MARK, SIM_MARK,
112              "Reply error-%s", whatsMyError());
113            }
114          break;
115
116        // unknown message token
117        default:
118          // reply error condition to sender
119          out->token = ERROR;
120          msgSize = sizeof(int);
121          if (Reply(sender, out, msgSize) == -1)
122            {
123            fcLogx(__FILE__, fn, SIM_MARK, SIM_MARK,
124              "Reply error-%s", whatsMyError());
125            }
126          fcLogx(__FILE__, fn, SIM_MARK, SIM_MARK,
127            "unknown token=%d", in->token);
128          break;
129        }
130    } // end of while loop
131
132  // program is finished
133  fcLogx(__FILE__, fn, globalMask, SIM_MARK, "done");
134
135  // remove SIMPL attachments
136  name_detach();
137
138  // exit gracefully
139  exit(0);
140  }
```

lines 2-6 Required standard 'C' headers.

lines 9-13 Headers described above. Note the use of _ALLOC in determining
   the extern status of global variables used in multiple source code files.

line 16 Required SIMPL definitions.

lines 19-22 Required headers for use with trace logger function calls.

lines 29-36 Local to main() variable declarations.

line 39 All required initialization procedures are performed here including the all-important SIMPL **name_attach**. The readies the program for SIMPL communications regardless of whether the program sends, receives or both. This initialize() function source is contained in the simInit.c file.

line 42 Inform the trace logger that the sim is starting.

lines 44-130 An infinite loop indicating that messages are to be received, processed and replied to indefinitely.

lines 47-53 The **Receive** blocks until a message arrives. The sender's SIMPL identity is pointed to by *sender*, the message is placed into the memory pointed to by *inArea* and the message cannot be any larger than the memory area indicated by *MAX_MSG_SIZE*. Note the error checking.

lines 56-128 We look at the value of the incoming message token in order to decide on the correct course of action. Note the switch default which catches errors in the token value.

lines 64,93 A solution to the incoming puzzle is attempted via the process() function call.

lines 80,109,121 The reply message is sent to the sender program. The message contents are set based on the findings of process() function or due to a bad message token.

The error handling in a stim or a sim is crucial because the point of sims and stims is to test the veracity of the SIMPL communications involved. The balance of the important sim code is as follows:

```
1  int process(SUDOKU_MSG *in, SUDOKU_MSG *out)
2  {
3  // datapath is global, set in initialize()
4  // size is global, set in main()
5  // array is global, set in readData()
6  int ret = FAIL;
7  char file[200];
8
```

```
9   // make the data file path and name
10  sprintf(file, "%s/valid_%d.dat", datapath, size);
11
12  // read in the required data file into the global array
13  readData(file);
14
15  // is the given puzzle the same as that sent in by stim?
16  if (!memcmp(array, in->elements, size * size))
17    {
18    // make the data file path and name
19    sprintf(file, "%s/answer_%d.dat", datapath, size);
20    // set the canned answer
21    readData(file);
22    memcpy(out->elements, array, size * size);
23    ret = SUCCESS;
24    }
25
26  return(ret);
27  }
```

line 10 The path and file name containing the corresponding message element array data is set; it contains either the 9x9 or 16x16 array of canned values.

line 13 The data file of canned values is read into memory.

lines 16-24 The canned file data is compared to the incoming array of canned data and if it compares favourably, then the *canned* solution is read from another data file and loaded into the reply message.

Note that there is no actual processing in the sim, that is not its purpose. We will be able to send a predefined canned message to the sim from either the GUI or the stim and test that the message data arrives in an uncorrupted state. In fact, we will be able to send predefined failures as well in order to check error handling logic.

13.5   Stimulator Logic

As discussed earlier, the purpose of the stimulator is to act as a SIMPL stub for the GUI (a SIMPL sender in our first cut design). In many ways, the stim looks like a mirror reflection of its SIMPL partner the sim. We will first use our stimulator to unit test the sim and eventually the engine. Let's take a look at the code for the stim starting with its headers followed by the code body.

stim.h

```
1   // defined macros
2   #define  SIZE_9        9
3   #define  SIZE_16       16
4   #define  SUCCESS       0
5   #define  FAIL          -1
6   #define  MAX_MSG_SIZE   1024
7
8   // for the logger
9   #define  STIM_MARK      0x00000001
10  #define  STIM_FUNC_IO   0x00000002
11  #define  STIM_MISC      0x00000010
12
13  // global variables
14  _ALLOC char myName[20]; // SIMPL name
15  _ALLOC int recvID; // SIMPL ID
16  _ALLOC int size; // size of the incoming puzzle (9x9 or 16x16)
17  _ALLOC int type; // anticipated from  receiver
18  _ALLOC char array[SIZE_16 * SIZE_16 + 1]; // maximum size
19  _ALLOC unsigned int globalMask; // for the logger
20  _ALLOC int backgroundMode; // to enable keyboard access
21  _ALLOC char datapath[80];
22  _ALLOC int fd;
23  _ALLOC int maxfd;
24  _ALLOC int my_fds[1];
25  _ALLOC fd_set watchset;
26  _ALLOC fd_set inset;
27
28  // for the incoming and outgoing messages
29  _ALLOC char inArea[MAX_MSG_SIZE];
30  _ALLOC char outArea[MAX_MSG_SIZE];
```

lines 2-6 Definitions used by sim code.

lines 9-11 Definitions used in trace logger function calls.

lines 14-26 Global variable declarations.

lines 29-30 Global incoming and outgoing message buffer declarations.

stimProto.h

```
1   void initialize(int, char **);
2   void myUsage(void);
```

```
3  char *skipOverWhiteSpace(char *);
4  void makeMsg(char *, SUDOKU_MSG *);
5  void checkMsg(SUDOKU_MSG *);
6  void readData(char *);
7  void printArray(void);
```

lines 1-7 Function prototype declarations.

line 1 All program initializations are carried out in this function at startup.

line 2 Program usage in the case of an incorrect command line.

line 3 A function used for parsing data.

line 4 The function that composes the outgoing message.

line 4 The function that checks the replied message.

line 5 The function that reads the appropriate data file.

line 6 The function that renders the Sudoku puzzle and its answer.

stim.c

```
1   // standard headers
2   #include <stdio.h>
3   #include <stdlib.h>
4   #include <unistd.h>
5   #include <time.h>
6   #include <string.h>
7   #include <dirent.h>
8
9   // stim program headers
10  #define _ALLOC
11  #include "stim.h"
12  #undef _ALLOC
13  #include "engineMsgs.h"
14  #include "stimProto.h"
15
16  // SIMPL headers
17  #include "simpl.h"
18
19  // for the logger
20  #define _ALLOC
21  #include "loggerVars.h"
```

```
22  #undef _ALLOC
23  #include "loggerProto.h"
24
25  /*=======================================
26    stim − entry point
27  ======================================*/
28  int main(int argc, char **argv, char **envp)
29  {
30  static char *fn = "stim";
31  int x_it = 0;
32  char line[80];
33  SUDOKU_MSG *in = (SUDOKU_MSG *)inArea;
34  SUDOKU_MSG *out = (SUDOKU_MSG *)outArea;
35  int msgSize;
36
37  // initialize variables, ready program for SIMPL communications etc.
38  initialize(argc, argv);
39
40  while (!x_it) // loop indefinitely
41      {
42      inset = watchset;
43      select(maxfd, &inset, NULL, NULL, NULL);
44
45      // is this from the keyboard?
46      if (FD_ISSET(my_fds[0], &inset))
47          {
48          fgets(line, 79, stdin);
49          line[strlen(line) − 1] = 0;
50
51          switch (line[0])
52              {
53              // help
54              case '?':
55                  printf("stimulator commands:\n");
56                  printf("f <puzzlefile> − send a test puzzle\n");
57                  printf("l − list test puzzles\n");
58                  printf("q − quit\n");
59                  break;
60
61              // compose and send test puzzle
62              case 'f':
63                  {
64                  char *p;
65                  p = skipOverWhiteSpace(line);
66
67                  // build message going to sim/engine
```

```
68          makeMsg(p, out);
69
70          // send the message
71          msgSize = sizeof(int) + size * size * sizeof(char);
72          if (Send(recvID, out, in, msgSize, msgSize) == -1)
73              {
74              fcLogx(__FILE__, fn, STIM_MARK, STIM_MARK,
75                  "%s: cannot send-%s\n", fn, whatsMyError());
76              printf("%s: cannot send-%s\n", fn, whatsMyError());
77              exit(-1);
78              }
79
80          // check reply from sim/engine
81          checkMsg(in);
82          }
83          break;
84
85      // list test puzzles
86      case 'l':
87          {
88          DIR *dir;
89          struct dirent *mydirent;
90
91          dir = opendir(datapath);
92          if (dir != NULL)
93              {
94              while ((mydirent = readdir(dir)) != NULL)
95                  {
96                  if ( (mydirent->d_name[0] != '.')
97                     && (mydirent->d_name[0] != 'C') )
98                      {
99                      printf("%s\n", mydirent->d_name);
100                     }
101                 }
102             }
103         }
104         break;
105
106     // quit
107     case 'q':
108         x_it = 1;
109         break;
110
111     default:
112         printf("%s: unknown keypress <%c>\n", fn, line[0]);
113         break;
```

```
114          }
115
116      printf("-> ");
117      fflush(stdout);
118      }
119   } // end of while loop
120
121 // program is finished
122 fcLogx(__FILE__, fn, globalMask, STIM_MISC, "done");
123
124 // remove SIMPL attachments
125 name_detach();
126
127 // exit gracefully
128 exit(0);
129 }
```

lines 2-7 Required standard 'C' headers.

lines 10-14 Headers described above. Note the use of _ALLOC in determining
    the extern status of global variables used in multiple source code files.

line 17 Required SIMPL definitions.

lines 20-23 Required headers for use with trace logger function calls. .

lines 30-35 Local to main() variable declarations.

line 38 All required initialization procedures are performed here including the
    all-important SIMPL *name_attach*. As well, stim is a sender and so the
    name_locate call for the receiver program is also present. The initialize()
    function source is contained in the stimInit.c file.

lines 40-119 An infinite loop indicating that the canned messages are to be
    selected by the user and sent to the receiver, processed and the reply dealt
    with indefinitely.

lines 42-49 This code deals with receiving instructions from the user via the
    keyboard.

lines 51-114 The keyboard entries being:

    1. ? -help

    2. f -the canned message to be sent

3. l -a list of the canned file messages that may be sent

4. q -quit the program

line 68 The makeMsg() function builds the desired outgoing message to the receiver.

line 71 The size of the message is determined. This is necessary for the **Send** function call. Since the reply message is of the same structure, the same value for size will be passed in as the expected reply message size.

lines 72-78 The canned message is sent to the receiver using the SIMPL identification number, the message to the receiver is pointed to by *out*, the anticipated reply message is pointed to by *in* and both the sent and replied message sizes are given by *msgSize*.

line 81 The replied message from the receiver is handled by the function checkMsg().

Let's finish up by looking at the balance of the pertinent code contained in stim.c.

```
1  void makeMsg(char *filename , SUDOKU_MSG *out)
2  {
3  // size is global
4  // type is global
5  // array is global
6  char *me = "stim";
7  char file[80];
8
9  // make the file path and name
10 sprintf(file , "%s/%s" , datapath , filename);
11
12 // use data file name to decide on the course of action taken
13 if (!strcmp(filename , "valid_9.dat"))
14    {
15    // set the token value
16    out->token = DO_9;
17    // for the message size
18    size = SIZE_9;
19    // type of reply message expected
20    type = DO_9;
21
22    // read the required data into the global array
23    readData(file);
24
25    // for the message
```

```
26      memcpy(out->elements, array, size * size);
27      }
28   else if (!strcmp(filename, "invalid_9.dat"))
29      {
30      // set the token value
31      out->token = DO_9;
32      // for the message size
33      size = SIZE_9;
34      // type of reply message expected
35      type = PUZZLE_FAILURE;
36
37      // for the message
38      memset(out->elements, 0, size * size);
39      }
40   else if (!strcmp(filename, "broken_9.dat"))
41      {
42      // set an invalid token
43      out->token = BAD_TOKEN;
44      // for the message size
45      size = SIZE_9;
46      // type of reply message expected
47      type = ERROR;
48      /*
49      we do not bother setting the values of the element array
50      and so we will be sending garbage, but it doesn't matter
51      because sim or engine should catch the bad token value first
52      */
53      }
54   else if (!strcmp(filename, "valid_16.dat"))
55      {
56      // set the token value
57      out->token = DO_16;
58      // for the message size
59      size = SIZE_16;
60      // type of reply message expected
61      type = DO_16;
62
63      // read the required data into the global array
64      readData(file);
65
66      // for the message
67      memcpy(out->elements, array, size * size);
68      }
69   else if (!strcmp(filename, "invalid_16.dat"))
70      {
71      // set the token value
```

```
72    out->token = DO_16;
73    // for the message size
74    size = SIZE_16;
75    // type of reply message expected
76    type = PUZZLE_FAILURE;
77
78    // for the message
79    memset(out->elements, 0, size * size);
80    }
81  else if (!strcmp(filename, "broken_16.dat"))
82    {
83    // set an invalid token
84    out->token = BAD_TOKEN;
85    // for the message size
86    size = SIZE_16;
87    // type of reply message expected
88    type = ERROR;
89    /*
90    we do not bother setting the values of the element array
91    and so we will be sending garbage, but it doesn't matter
92    because sim or engine should catch the bad token value first
93    */
94    }
95  else
96    {
97    printf("%s: file name %s is non-sequitor\n", me, filename);
98    exit(-1);
99    }
100 }
```

line 10 The name and path of the canned message file is set.

lines 32-94 Based on the input data file name, we set the size of the puzzle, the message token, the expected reply type (DO_9 or DO_16 for success, PUZZLE_FAILURE for failure and ERROR for a bad token) and the puzzle element array values as necessary.

```
1  void checkMsg(SUDOKU_MSG *in)
2  {
3  // size is global
4  // type is global
5  char answerFile[200];
6
7  // the expected incoming token and the type should match
8  if (in->token != type)
```

```
 9      {
10      printf("Problem: type=%d != token=%d\n", type, in->token);
11      return;
12      }
13
14  switch (in->token)
15      {
16      case DO_9:
17        // success
18        // print outgoing array of numbers
19        printf("\nSent puzzle\n");
20        printArray();
21        sprintf(answerFile, "%s/%s", datapath, "answer_9.dat");
22        // read in the canned answer
23        readData(answerFile);
24        // compare the canned answer to the replied solution
25        if (!memcmp(array, in->elements, size * size))
26          {
27          printf("Successful answer-communications intact.\n");
28          printArray();
29          }
30        else
31          {
32          printf("Unsuccessful answer-communication problems?\n");
33          }
34        break;
35
36      case DO_16:
37        // success
38        // print outgoing array of numbers
39        printf("\nSent puzzle\n");
40        printArray();
41        sprintf(answerFile, "%s/%s", datapath, "answer_16.dat");
42        // read in the canned answer
43        readData(answerFile);
44        // compare the canned answer to the replied solution
45        if (!memcmp(array, in->elements, size * size))
46          {
47          printf("Successful answer-communications appear intact.\n");
48          printArray();
49          }
50        else
51          {
52          printf("Unsuccessful answer-communication problems?\n");
53          }
54        break;
```

```
55
56    case ERROR:
57        // sent token is bad or other problem
58        printf("Token failure: which is the correct response.\n");
59        break;
60
61    case PUZZLE_FAILURE:
62        // an invalid puzzle
63        printf("Puzzle failure: which is the correct response.\n");
64        break;
65
66    default:
67        printf("Invalid reply token.\n");
68        break;
69    }
70 }
```

lines 8-12 The reply token is checked to see if it is the expected value. If not, there is a real problem and not a planned one.

lines 14-68 The veracity of the replied message is checked to ensure that the programs are functioning properly and that the message passing is working correctly.

13.6 Testing Sim and Stim

In this section we would like to run the simulator and stimulator programs together. Once things are compiled and linked we will have the sim and stim binaries respectively. We want to unit test the two programs with each other so that we can verify their abilities to handle normal and abnormal situations.

Unfortunately, unit testing sim and stim could be a confliction in terms. We must test both with one and other. When we are satisfied that they both work correctly, then we can use them to unit test the GUI programs and the engine. Our testing for sim and stim can be pictured in Figure 11.1. We have previously defined this test to be *sb000*.

Test **sb000** is concerned with checking various aspects of the message passing between stim and sim. The tests we are going to run are as follows:

1. Sending a valid 9x9 canned message and replying a valid canned response.

2. Sending an invalid 9x9 message via corrupt puzzle element data, simulating message corruption, and replying a failure.

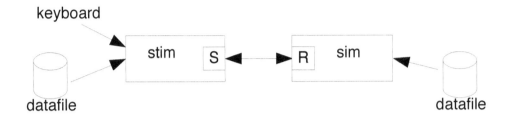

Figure 13.1: Sim/Stim SIMPL Test sb000

3. Sending an invalid 9x9 message via an unknown token.

4. Sending a valid 16x16 canned message and replying a valid response.

5. Sending an invalid 16x16 message via corrupt puzzle element data and replying a failure.

6. Sending an invalid 16x16 message via an unknown token.

In *test 1* we are going to send the canned 9x9 puzzle clues to the sim and expect the appropriate canned solution by replied message. We expect success and if success is the response, well and good. If not, there may be a problem with the contents of the message structure or how it is loaded or how it is read. Perhaps there is even a problem with the logic in one or both sim and stim. There may even be a problem with the way the token is set by stim and interpreted by sim. Another probable area for problems is the memory logic pertaining to the messages.

In *test 2* we are sending a message with bad 9x9 data. We expect a reply message containing a failure.

In *test 3* we are deliberately sending a 9x9 message with an unknown message token and verifying that the sim program handles it correctly.

In *test 4* we are simply repeating case 1 but with a 16x16 puzzle and so we are then exercising that particular logic stream.

In *test 5* we are sending a message with bad 16x16 data. We expect a reply message containing a failure.

In *test 6* we are deliberately sending a 16x16 message with an unknown message token and verifying that the sim program handles it correctly.

Recall from Chapter 8 describing the SIMPL testing framework that we view all tests as being composed of three stages, each represented by a wrapper script.

> 1. pretest - The setup of the testing environment.
> 2. dotest - The actual execution of the test.
> 3. posttest - The examination of the results.

In this test (sb000) we don't require the first wrapper script called pretest because there is no special setup required. Accordingly, the following two command scripts will fulfill the sb000 test procedure:

- dotest sb000

- posttest sb000

dotest: The dotest script performs the actual tests by running sim and stim via the *runtest* file. The runtest file appears as follows:

```
#!/bin/bash

TEST_NO=sb000
TEST_DESC="sim/stim unit test"

TEST_DIR=$TEST_HOME/testing/test$TEST_NO
OUTFILE=$TEST_DIR/results/test.out

echo "Starting up test #$TEST_NO" |tee $OUTFILE
echo $TEST_DESC | tee -a $OUTFILE
date | tee -a $OUTFILE

cd $SIMPL_HOME/bin
fclogger -n LOGGER > $TEST_DIR/results/junk &

cd $TEST_HOME/sudoku/bin
sim -n SIM -p $TEST_DIR/data -l LOGGER &
sleep 1
stim -n STIM -r SIM -p $TEST_DIR/data -l LOGGER |tee -a $OUTFILE

fcslay SIM
fcslay LOGGER

echo "Test finished you can run posttest $TEST_NO for result"
```

As you can see by inspecting the above coded instructions, sim is run in the background, stim is run in foreground, and the output of the programs is written to an output file called test.out.

posttest: Finally, by running posttest the contents of the dotest output file *test.out* can be examined. When we are certain that both the sim and the stim handle all their messages correctly, we will then be in a position to use them as a starting point for developing the engine and the GUI programs respectively and to act as test stubs for the engine and GUI program unit tests.

13.7   Summary

In this chapter we have constructed the simulator (sim) and stimulator (stim) stub programs derived from the softwareICs repository code. We have modified the repository code to fit the requirements of the Sudoku software. We have plumbed out our *unit* test (sb000) for the sim and stim to verify that they function correctly. As a developer's personal SIMPL toolbox grows, reliance on the softwareICs repository will decrease.

13.8   Next Chapter

In the next chapter we are going to take the functional sim code and port it easily to the fully functional Sudoku engine program. We will then use the stim to unit test the engine.

Chapter 14

Sudoku Engine Program

In this chapter we are going to describe the process for writing the Sudoku engine program code. We will leverage off our previous work on the sim. By adopting this process, we can be relatively certain that the SIMPL aspect of the engine code will be functional at the start. The engine can be fully tested with our stim. The GUI programming can proceed independently because it can be unit tested with the sim.

14.1   Building the Engine Program

What is missing from the sim code that we require for the engine? The answer is the parts that have nothing to do with SIMPL. By adding the problem solving algorithm to the sim we should have the complete engine. We are not going to discuss the algorithm used by the engine to solve Sudoku puzzles in any detail. Suffice to say that the code first tries to solve the puzzle deterministically if there is enough information. If not, then guesses are made recursively after the last point of certitude. The code for this algorithm is freely available on the SIMPL book website.[1]

Let's take a look at the engine code here. It helps to look back at the sim code and note how the sim code has formed the framework for the engine program. We will start with *engine.h* and *engineProto.h* which are the header files containing relevant definitions, global variables, and function prototypes.

---

[1]If you wish to follow along with some real code in front of you the entire Sudoku project code is available at **http://www.icanprogram.com/simplBook**.

engine.h

```
1   // defined macros
2   #define SIZE_9          9
3   #define SIZE_16         16
4   #define SUB_SIZE_9      3
5   #define SUB_SIZE_16     4
6   #define SPACE           ' '
7   #define FIRST           1
8   #define ALL             0
9   #define MAX_GUESSES     3
10  #define MAX_MSG_SIZE    1024
11
12  // for the logger
13  #define RECV_MARK       0x00000001
14  #define RECV_FUNC_IO    0x00000002
15  #define RECV_MISC       0x00000010
16
17  typedef struct
18      {
19      int number;
20      int place[SIZE_16]; // maximum possible size
21      } POSSIBILITY;
22
23  // global variables
24  _ALLOC int size; // size of the incoming puzzle (9x9 or 16x16)
25  _ALLOC char array[SIZE_16 * SIZE_16]; // maximum size
26  _ALLOC int subSize; // incoming puzzle's submatrix size (3x3 or 4x4)
27  _ALLOC char numbers_9[SIZE_9]; // possible values for 9x9
28  _ALLOC char numbers_16[SIZE_16]; // possible values for 16x16
29  _ALLOC char *numbers; // pointer to a number array
30  _ALLOC unsigned int globalMask; // for the logger
31
32  // for the incoming and outgoing messages
33  _ALLOC char inArea[MAX_MSG_SIZE];
34  _ALLOC char outArea[MAX_MSG_SIZE];
```

lines 2-10 Definitions used by engine code.

lines 13-15 Definitions used in trace logger function calls.

lines 24-30 Global variable declarations.

lines 33-34 Global incoming and outgoing message buffer declarations.

engineProto.h

```
1   void initialize(int, char **);
2   void myUsage(void);
3   int doCalculations(void);
4   int process(void);
5   int checkArray(void);
6   int doExact(void);
7   int doRows(void);
8   int doColumns(void);
9   int doSubs(void);
10  int findRowPosition(int, char);
11  int findColumnPosition(int, char);
12  int findSubPosition(int, int, char, int *, int *);
13  int doInexact(int);
14  void getPossibilities(int, char, POSSIBILITY *);
15  int findCharacter(int, int, char, int);
16  int checkValues(void);
17  int runTest(int);
18  void printArray(void);
19  void initialize_1(void);
20  void initialize_2(void);
21  void initialize_3(void);
22  void initialize_4(void);
23  void initialize_5(void);
24  void initialize_6(void);
25  void initialize_7(void);
26  void initialize_8(void);
```

lines 1-26 Function prototype declarations.

engine.c

```
1   // standard headers
2   #include <stdio.h>
3   #include <stdlib.h>
4   #include <unistd.h>
5   #include <time.h>
6   #include <string.h>
7
8   // engine program headers
9   #define _ALLOC
10  #include "engine.h"
11  #undef _ALLOC
12  #include "engineMsgs.h"
```

```
13  #include "engineProto.h"
14
15  // SIMPL headers
16  #include "simpl.h"
17
18  // for the logger
19  #define _ALLOC
20  #include "loggerVars.h"
21  #undef _ALLOC
22  #include "loggerProto.h"
23
24  /*===========================================================
25    engine - entry point
26  ===========================================================*/
27  int main(int argc, char **argv, char **envp)
28  {
29  static char *fn = "engine";
30  int x_it = 0;
31  int nbytes;
32  char *sender;
33  SUDOKU_MSG *in = (SUDOKU_MSG *)inArea;
34  SUDOKU_MSG *out = (SUDOKU_MSG *)outArea;
35  int msgSize;
36  int ret;
37
38  // initialize variables, SIMPL etc.
39  initialize(argc, argv);
40
41  // log the startup
42  fcLogx(__FILE__, fn, globalMask, RECV_MARK, "starting");
43
44  while (!x_it)
45    {
46    // receive incoming messages
47    nbytes = Receive(&sender, inArea, MAX_MSG_SIZE);
48    if (nbytes == -1)
49      {
50      fcLogx(__FILE__, fn, RECV_MARK, RECV_MARK,
51        "Receive error-%s", whatsMyError());
52      continue;
53      }
54
55    // decide course of action based on value of the message token
56    switch (in->token)
57      {
58      // a 9x9 puzzle
```

```
59   case DO_9:
60       // set necessary variables
61       size = SIZE_9;
62       subSize = SUB_SIZE_9;
63       memcpy(array, in->elements, SIZE_9 * SIZE_9);
64       numbers = numbers_9;
65
66       // try to solve the puzzle and compose reply message
67       ret = doCalculations();
68       if (ret != -1)
69           {
70           // success
71           out->token = DO_9;
72           memcpy(out->elements, array, size * size);
73           // use msgSize NOT sizeof(MSG), C may pad out structure
74           msgSize = sizeof(int) + size * size * sizeof(char);
75           }
76       else
77           {
78           // failure
79           out->token = PUZZLE_FAILURE;
80           msgSize = sizeof(int);
81           }
82
83       // reply results to sender
84       if (Reply(sender, out, msgSize) == -1)
85           {
86           fcLogx(__FILE__, fn, RECV_MARK, RECV_MARK,
87               "Reply error-%s", whatsMyError());
88           }
89       break;
90
91   // a 16x16 puzzle
92   case DO_16:
93       // set necessary variables
94       size = SIZE_16;
95       subSize = SUB_SIZE_16;
96       memcpy(array, in->elements, SIZE_16 * SIZE_16);
97       numbers = numbers_16;
98
99       // try to solve the puzzle and compose reply message
100      ret = doCalculations();
101      if (ret != -1)
102          {
103          // success
104          out->token = DO_16;
```

```
105            memcpy(out->elements, array, size * size);
106            // use msgSize NOT sizeof(MSG), C may pad out structure
107            msgSize = sizeof(int) + size * size * sizeof(char);
108            }
109        else
110            {
111            // failure
112            out->token = PUZZLE_FAILURE;
113            msgSize = sizeof(int);
114            }
115
116        // reply results to sender
117        if (Reply(sender, out, msgSize) == -1)
118            {
119            fcLogx(__FILE__, fn, RECV_MARK, RECV_MARK,
120                "Reply error-%s", whatsMyError());
121            }
122        break;
123
124      // unknown message token
125      default:
126        // reply error condition to sender
127        out->token = ERROR;
128        msgSize = sizeof(int);
129        if (Reply(sender, out, msgSize) == -1)
130            {
131            fcLogx(__FILE__, fn, RECV_MARK, RECV_MARK,
132                "Reply error-%s", whatsMyError());
133            }
134        fcLogx(__FILE__, fn, RECV_MARK, RECV_MARK,
135            "unknown token=%d", in->token);
136        break;
137      }
138    }
139
140 // program is finished
141 fcLogx(__FILE__, fn, globalMask, RECV_MARK, "done");
142
143 // remove SIMPL attachments
144 name_detach();
145
146 // exit gracefully
147 exit(0);
148 }
```

lines 2-6 Required standard 'C' headers.

lines 9-13 Headers described above. Note the use of _ALLOC in determining the extern status of global variables used in multiple source code files.

line 16 Required SIMPL definitions.

lines 19-22 Required headers for use with trace logger function calls.

lines 29-36 Local to main() variable declarations.

line 39 All required initialization procedures are performed here including the all-important SIMPL **name_attach**. The initialize() function source is contained in the engineInit.c file.

line 42 Inform the trace logger that the engine is starting.

lines 44-138 An infinite loop indicating that messages are to be received, processed and replied to indefinitely.

lines 47-53 The **Receive** blocks until a message arrives. The sender's SIMPL identity is pointed to by *sender*, the message is placed into the memory pointed to by *inArea* and the message cannot be any larger than the memory area indicated by *MAX_MSG_SIZE*. Note the error checking.

lines 56-138 We look at the value of the incoming message token in order to decide on the correct course of action. Note the switch default which catches errors in the token value.

lines 67,100 A solution to the incoming puzzle is attempted via the doCalculation() function call.

lines 84,117,129 The reply message is sent to the sender program via **Reply**. The message contents are set based on the findings of doCalculation() function or due to a bad message token.

Comparing this code to the sim code shows a line for line correlation at many points. Many SIMPL projects are evolved in exactly this manner; clone some existing code and modify it to suit. The real functional differences between the engine and the sim code are largely isolated in the transition from the **process** call in sim.c to the **doCalculation** call in engine.c.

Here is a quick look at the rest of the more relevant engine code.

pertinent engine.c code

```
 1  int doCalculations(void)
 2  {
 3  // check incoming puzzle values
 4  if (checkValues() == -1)
 5    {
 6    return(-1);
 7    }
 8
 9  // let's try determinism
10  if (doExact() == 0)
11    {
12    return(0);
13    }
14
15  // let's make a guess
16  if (doInexact(MAX_GUESSES) == 0)
17    {
18    return(0);
19    }
20
21  return(-1);
22  }
```

lines 4-7 The checkValues() function checks the incoming element data for inconsistencies.

lines 10-13 The doExact() function is the entry point for attempting a strictly deterministic solution to the puzzle.

lines 16-19 The doInexact() function tries to arrive at a solution through a series of recursive guesses if the deterministic method fails.

The code for doExact() and doInexact() are not printed in this book as they have nothing directly to do with SIMPL. The code can be found in the engineUtils.c file available in the source tarball.

14.2   Testing the Engine

Supposing at this point that we have an engine program that compiles and links, we are now ready for unit testing with the stim. Unit testing the engine can be pictured in Figure 14.1.

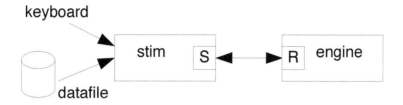

Figure 14.1: Engine Unit Test sb001

Test **sb001** is concerned with checking various aspects of the message passing between stimulator and engine. These tests are identical to the sim/stim tests in the previous chapter. Stim will test the SIMPL functionality of the engine. Moreover, unlike sim which had canned responses, the engine will have to solve the valid puzzles sent to it. For completeness we repeat some of the verbage in the sim/stim chapter with respect to the various tests we will employ.

1. Sending a valid 9x9 canned message and replying a solution.

2. Sending an invalid 9x9 message via corrupt puzzle element data, simulating message corruption, and replying a failure.

3. Sending an invalid 9x9 message via an unknown token.

4. Sending a valid 16x16 canned message and replying a solution.

5. Sending an invalid 16x16 message via corrupt puzzle element data and replying a failure.

6. Sending an invalid 16x16 message via an unknown token.

In *test 1* we are going to send the canned 9x9 puzzle clues to the engine and expect a puzzle answer which should correspond to the canned solution by replied message. We expect success and if success is the response then the Sudoku engine is able to solve puzzles. If not, there may be a problem with the contents of the message structure or how it is loaded or how it is read or our puzzle engine is actually disfunctional. Another probable area for problems is the memory logic pertaining to the messages.

In *test 2* we are sending a message with bad 9x9 data. We expect a reply message containing a failure.

In *test 3* we are deliberately sending a 9x9 message with an unknown message token and verifying that the engine program handles it correctly. This should work immediately because it is the same code as in the sim program.

In *test 4* we are simply repeating test 1 but with a 16x16 puzzle and so we are then exercising that particular logic stream.

In *test 5* we are sending a message with bad 16x16 data. We expect a reply message containing a failure.

In *test 6* we are deliberately sending a 16x16 message with an unknown message token and verifying that the engine program handles it correctly.

As in the sim/stim chapter, the following command scripts comprise test sb001:

- dotest sb001

- posttest sb001

<u>*dotest:*</u> The dotest script performs the actual tests by running engine and stim via the *runtest* file. The runtest file appears as follows:

```
#!/bin/bash

TEST_NO=sb001
TEST_DESC="engine unit test"

TEST_DIR=$TEST_HOME/testing/test$TEST_NO
OUTFILE=$TEST_DIR/results/test.out

echo "Starting up test #$TEST_NO" |tee $OUTFILE
echo $TEST_DESC | tee -a $OUTFILE
date | tee -a $OUTFILE

cd $SIMPL_HOME/bin
fclogger -n LOGGER > $TEST_DIR/results/junk &

cd $TEST_HOME/sudoku/bin
engine -n ENGINE -l LOGGER &
sleep 1
stim -n STIM -r ENGINE -p $TEST_DIR/data -l LOGGER |tee -a $OUTFILE

fcslay ENGINE
fcslay LOGGER

echo "Test finished you can run posttest $TEST_NO for result"
```

Again, as in the stim/sim test you can see by inspecting the above coded instructions that engine is run in the background, stim is run in foreground, and the output of the programs is written to an output file called test.out.

posttest: Running posttest, the contents of the dotest output file *test.out* may be examined. When we are satisfied that engine works adequately, we are now in a position to move on to looking at the GUI programming.[2]

14.3   Self Test

We stated earlier that the actual processing code for the Sudoku engine is not included in the book. However, for those interested in testing this code there is a self-test capability inherent in the engine software. The self-test code is called from the engineInit.c file through function call runTest(). The self-test is activated when the engine is run in standalone mode and is started from the command line as follows:

   engine -t num

where num=1-8. These numbers represent various tests, some of which are quite difficult and may require several minutes to solve.

14.4   Summary

In this chapter we built the Sudoku engine program based directly on the sim program software. We also based its unit test *sb001* on the unit test used for the sim and stim, sb000. If all is well we have a fully functioning Sudoku engine that is capable of solving 9x9 and 16x16 puzzles. We are now in a position to move on to the GUI software.

14.5   Next Chapter

In the next chapter we are going to develop the Python GUI secure in the knowledge that we have functional sim and engine receivers with which to measure our new GUI software against.

---

[2]Samples of these testing framework scripts can be found in the project tarball for the Sudoku project code at **http://www.icanprogram.com/simplBook**.

Chapter 15

Python/Tk GUI

Our hypothetical engine development team has been able to evolve the simulator code through a logical progression of stages into our Sudoku puzzle engine. They were able to do this in part because they had a capable GUI stub in the form of a stimulator to exercise the engine code changes as they were developed. The Python GUI team will not get off as easily. While the stimulator code is functionally the same as what the GUI will require, it is written in a very different style (procedural vs. OOP) and in a very different programming language ('C' vs. Python). Furthermore, the SIMPL messaging aspects of our Python GUI will likely only form a minor portion of the actual code. As such the GUI team will not be able to use the stimulator as seed code and evolve it in a logical progression into their GUI solution. What the Python GUI team does have going for it however, is the fact that they need not concern themselves with any aspect of the engine algorithm other than conforming to the SIMPL messaging interface embodied by the sim. These SIMPL aspects of the GUI code will be straightforward and the GUI team will be able to code and debug these early on and spend the bulk of their effort on the GUI itself.

As with most GUI code, the bulk of the lines of code will be concerned with interface details such as window/widget size and position. More details are involved with displaying a GUI representation of the Sudoku puzzle than were needed for the straight stimulator test stub. Font selection, point size, colour schemes and widget layout are just some of the things that the GUI design team needs to be working out. In addition, the GUI design team needs to be thinking about the human interface to the GUI as well. Things like how will the puzzle elements get entered and how the puzzle engine gets engaged need to be designed. As the team works through these items a proposed screen layout is the likely outcome.

There are many possible GUI interface *choices* for our puzzle solver. We have
deliberately chosen a very basic one. This is a book about SIMPL and not a book
about Python GUI programming after all. The important thing to remember
as you examine the details of our basic solution below is that all GUI solutions
will follow the basic SIMPL sender layout: *name_attach*, *name_locate*, *Send*
and process response. It is also important to remember that SIMPL and our
SIMPL Testing Framework has allowed the GUI team to completely isolate their
work from that of the engine team. The only point of interface between those
teams is in the tokenized SIMPL message definitions, which for the GUI team
are fully exercised by the sim. In more realistic real world projects this ability
to separate project teams is an important part of the SIMPL way.

15.1   Building the Python/Tk GUI

In this section we are going to examine the Python/Tk GUI code. Note that
much of the callback code has been left out in order to save space. This code is
available as part of the Sudoku source code tarball.[1]

gui.py

```
1   #! /usr/Python-2.5.1/python
2
3   # import necessary modules
4   import sys
5   import struct
6   import simpl
7   import psimpl
8   import tkMessageBox
9   from Tkinter import *
10
11  # define constants
12  DO_9=0
13  DO_16=1
14
15  # global variables
16  global matrixElements  # a series of button widgets
17  global size            # a 9X9 or 16X16 puzzle matrix
18  global numbers         # the possible puzzle values
19  global saved           # saved values for puzzles
20
21  """
```

---
[1]The Python/Tk code is available at http://www.icanprogram.com/simplBook

```
22   Many of the callbacks have been left out of the book.
23   They would normally appear in this area.
24   """
25   # a callback for the submit button
26   # take the button text and use to build the SIMPL message
27   def hndlSubmit ():
28     # why send an empty array?
29     if hndlCheck ():
30       tkMessageBox.showwarning ("Warning", "No non-blank elements")
31       return
32
33     # assemble the message
34     if size == 9:
35       outToken = DO_9
36     else:
37       outToken = DO_16
38
39     length = size * size
40     outElements = ""
41     inElements = ""
42     inToken = -1;
43
44     for cell in range(length):
45       outElements += matrixElements [cell]["text"]
46       inElements += matrixElements [cell]["text"]
47       saved [cell] = matrixElements [cell]["text"]
48       """
49       print ("cell=%d val=%s elements=%s"
50         %(cell, matrixElements [cell]["text"], outElements))
51       """
52     # set the outgoing message
53     oMsg = struct.pack("i" + str(length) + "s", outToken, outElements)
54
55     # initialize the incoming message
56     iMsg = struct.pack("i" + str(length) + "s", inToken, inElements)
57
58     """
59     # observe the outgoing message
60     t = psimpl.getBinaryValue(oMsg, 0, psimpl. SINT, "i")
61     s = psimpl.getBinaryValue(oMsg, psimpl.SINT, length, "s")
62     print ("t=%d s=%s" %(t, s))
63     """
64
65     # send the message
66     retVal = simpl.Send(receiverId, oMsg, iMsg)
67     if retVal == -1:
```

```
68        tkMessageBox.showerror("SIMPL send error", simpl.whatsMyError())
69        sys.exit(-1)
70
71     # process the reply message
72     inToken = psimpl.getBinaryValue(iMsg, 0, psimpl.SINT, "i")
73     inElements = psimpl.getBinaryValue(iMsg, psimpl.SINT, length, "s")
74
75     #print("t=%d s=%s" %(token, inElements))
76
77     # not a successful solution?
78     if inToken != outToken:
79       tkMessageBox.showwarning("Warning", "Problem solving puzzle")
80
81     # show results- sent values BLACK, calculated values RED
82     for cell in range(length):
83       matrixElements[cell]["text"] = inElements[cell]
84       if outElements[cell] == " ":
85         #print("blank cell=%d" %(cell))
86         matrixElements[cell]["foreground"] ="red"
87 #*********************************************************************
88
89 # operational start of the program
90
91 # what size of puzzle are we dealing with?
92 if len(sys.argv) != 4:
93   tkMessageBox.showerror("Incorrect command line")
94   sys.exit(-1)
95
96 # initialize some variables
97 sName = sys.argv[1] # this program's SIMPL name
98 rName = sys.argv[2] # the sim/engine program's SIMPL name
99 if sys.argv[3] == "16":# the puzzle size
100   size = 16
101 else:
102   size = 9
103 matrixElements = [None] * size * size # this puzzles elements
104 saved = [None] * size * size # saved values for matrix elements
105
106 # what characters are available for populating the puzzle?
107 if size == 16:
108   numbers = \
109     [" ","0","1","2","3","4","5","6","7","8","9","A","B",\
110     "C","D","E","F"]
111 else:
112   numbers = [" ","1","2","3","4","5","6","7","8","9"]
113
```

```
114  # attach the SIMPL name
115  retVal = simpl.name_attach(sName)
116  if retVal == -1:
117    err = simpl.whatsMyError() + ": check for another program instance"
118    tkMessageBox.showerror("SIMPL name attach error", err)
119    sys.exit(-1)
120
121  # name locate the C program SIMPL receiver
122  receiverId = simpl.name_locate(rName)
123  if receiverId == -1:
124    err = simpl.whatsMyError() + ": is the receiver program running?"
125    tkMessageBox.showerror("SIMPL name attach error", err)
126    sys.exit(-1)
127
128  # initialize Tk for graphics
129  root = Tk()
130
131  # the graphical matrix elements are to be buttons
132  for row in range(size):
133    rowframe = Frame(root)
134    rowframe.pack(fill=BOTH)
135    for column in range(size):
136      num = row * size + column
137      if size == 16:
138        myFont = ("Times", 30, "bold")
139      else:
140        myFont = ("Times", 40, "bold")
141      matrixElements[num] = Button(rowframe, borderwidth=1,
142        relief=SOLID, justify=CENTER, bg="White", fg="Black",
143        text=" ", font=myFont, width=2)
144      matrixElements[num].bind("<Button-1>", hndlIncrease)
145      matrixElements[num].bind("<Button-3>", hndlDecrease)
146      matrixElements[num].pack(side=LEFT)
147
148  # the bottom frame of buttons
149  rowframe = Frame(root)
150  rowframe.pack(fill=BOTH)
151  Button(rowframe, justify=CENTER, text="Help",
152    command=hndlHelp).pack(side=LEFT)
153  Button(rowframe, justify=CENTER, text="Clear",
154    command=hndlClear).pack(side=LEFT, expand=YES)
155  Button(rowframe, justify=CENTER, text="Save",
156    command=hndlSave).pack(side=LEFT, expand=YES)
157  Button(rowframe, justify=CENTER, text="Restore",
158    command=hndlRestore).pack(side=LEFT, expand=YES)
159  Button(rowframe, justify=CENTER, text="Test Puzzle",
```

```
160    command=hndlTest ).pack(side=LEFT, expand=YES)
161  Button(rowframe, justify=CENTER, text="Submit",
162    command=hndlSubmit ).pack(side=RIGHT)
163
164  # handle user input
165  root.mainloop()
```

line 1 Declares the location of the python interpreter to be used.

lines 4-9 Required imported modules. Note particularly the simpl and psimpl modules.

lines 12-13 Defined constants.

lines 16-19 Global variable declarations.

lines 27-86 The hndlSubmit callback. This callback has been included in the code listing because it is responsible for composing the message to be sent, sending the message, and then processing the reply.

lines 29-31 There is no point in sending an empty array for processing.

lines 34-56 Incoming and outgoing message values are set and preset.

lines 66-69 The outgoing message is sent and the replied message is returned.

lines 72-86 The replied message is processed.

lines 92-94 The command line is checked.

lines 97-112 Variable initializations.

lines 114-118 SIMPL *name_attach*.

lines 121-125 SIMPL *name_locate* of the receiving process.

line 128 Tk method is initialized.

lines 131-145 The sudoku puzzle matrix elements are drawn.

lines 148-161 The buttons are drawn.

line 164 Event loop is started for handling user input.

15.2   Testing the Python/Tk GUI

Now that we have a Python/Tk GUI program, we are now ready to unit test it
with the help of the sim program. Unit testing the Python GUI can be pictured
in Figure 15.1.

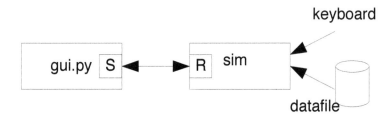

Figure 15.1: Python/Tk Unit Test sb002

Test *sb002* is concerned with checking the message passing between the
python GUI and the sim. Essentially, sb002 confirms that the GUI client functions correctly. From the earlier test sb000 we can be relatively certain that the
sim works correctly. This allows us an opportunity to work on the GUI program
knowing that any problems encountered are most likely due to the Python code.
For this test, we simply want to send the canned 9x9 and 16x16 messages to the
sim and observe the reply. In order to do this we run the following commands:

- pretest sb002

- dotest sb002

- posttest sb002

pretest: We have elected to dedicate the pretest script to choosing the size of
the puzzle to be tested, 9x9 or 16x16. Pretest is a wrapper script which points
to the *setup* file which looks like:

```
#!/bin/bash

TEST_NO=sb002
TEST_DESC="Python GUI unit test"

TEST_DIR=$TEST_HOME/testing/test$TEST_NO
DATA_DIR=$TEST_DIR/data
```

```
OUTFILE=$TEST_DIR/results/test.out

echo "Starting up test #$TEST_NO" | tee $OUTFILE
echo $TEST_DESC | tee -a $OUTFILE
date | tee -a $OUTFILE

echo ""
echo "======================================"
echo "1) 9x9 puzzle"
echo "2) 16x16 puzzle"
echo ""
echo -n "-> "
read ans

cd $TEST_DIR/data

if [ $ans == '1' ]
then
  if [ -f size16 ]
  then
    rm size16
  fi
else
  date > size16
fi

echo "Test $TEST_NO setup finished"
```

dotest: The dotest script performs the actual tests involving running the python GUI and the sim. The dotest script is itself a wrapper for the specific STF _runtest_ file. In the GUI interface, selecting the _Test Puzzle_ button should cause some of the matrix elements to be filled in automatically. These values represent the 9x9 or 16x16 canned test puzzle messages that the sim receives. The _Submit_ button activates the submission of this test puzzle to the engine stub (sim). The sim is designed to recognize this test puzzle and return a valid solution message. If any of the values in the test puzzle are altered, this is equivalent to sending an invalid message and the sim should respond with an error.

The runtest file appears as follows:

```
#!/bin/bash

TEST_NO=sb002
TEST_DESC="Python GUI unit test"
```

```
TEST_DIR=$TEST_HOME/testing/test$TEST_NO
OUTFILE=$TEST_DIR/results/test.out

echo "Starting up test #$TEST_NO" | tee $OUTFILE
echo $TEST_DESC | tee -a $OUTFILE
date | tee -a $OUTFILE

cd $SIMPL_HOME/bin
fclogger -n LOGGER > $TEST_DIR/results/junk &

cd $TEST_HOME/sudoku/bin
sim -n SIM -p $TEST_DIR/data -l LOGGER &
sleep 1

if [ -f $TEST_DIR/data/size16 ]
then
  SIZE=16
else
  SIZE=9
fi

python gui.py gui.py SIM $SIZE

fcslay SIM
fcslay LOGGER

echo "Test finished you can run posttest $TEST_NO for result"
```

During the execution of test sb002 the puzzle screen will appear something like Figure 15.2.

The posttest script isn't used in this test because most of the things you'd want to validate are visible only on the GUI screen itself. Internal errors detected by the sim will appear in the trace log.

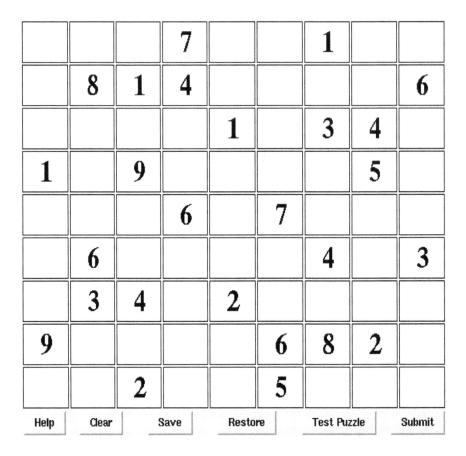

Figure 15.2: Python/Tk GUI screen

15.3   Summary

In this chapter we were given the Python GUI and unit tested it with the sim via test sb002. The number of tests was smaller because we have already ascertained that the sim can handle unknown tokens and the GUI tokens are contained within the code.

15.4   Next Chapter

In the next chapter we will perform the integration testing of the Python GUI with the engine because we have satisfactorily unit tested both the Python GUI and the engine programs.

Chapter 16

Integration Testing - Python GUI/ Sudoku Engine

Up to this point in the project we have exercised unit tests associated with the various SIMPL modules in our system. Once those modules are thoroughly unit tested, they need to be joined together as they would be deployed and integration tested in that configuration. Test sb004 represents the integration test with the Python GUI client and the Sudoku engine. See Figure 16.1

Figure 16.1: Python Integration test

The unit test sb002 validated that the Python client successfully composed a Sudoku puzzle message and submitted it to the engine simulator (sim). So at this stage we know that the client works. Likewise, we know that if the puzzle message is malformed the client correctly handles the error returned. Finally, the engine unit test has demonstrated that the engine can receive puzzles, solve them, and return the solution to the sender.

In the integration test we are interested in checking whether the two halves of the system join together correctly. We are also interested in investigating the performance of this system in realistic operating conditions. Integration tests are used to expose the system to the end users and to solicit their suggestions for improvements. During integration testing we would want to submit a range of puzzles to the system and observe the ensuing behaviour. Our *simplest system which works* initial design uses a blocking **Send** which will impact the feel of the GUI in cases where the puzzle solving engine is occupied for more than a few seconds. We would want to gauge user reaction in these cases.

This test will formally be run in the normal manner:

- pretest sb004

- dotest sb004

- posttest sb004

The pretest script will allow the tester to decide the size of the puzzle to displayed, 9x9 or 16x16 just as in the unit test (sb002). (see Chapter 15).

The dotest script for sb004 would look something like the version below.

```bash
#!/bin/bash

TEST_NO=sb004
TEST_DESC="integration test with Python GUI"

TEST_DIR=$TEST_HOME/testing/test$TEST_NO
OUTFILE=$TEST_DIR/results/test.out

echo "Starting up test #$TEST_NO" | tee $OUTFILE
echo $TEST_DESC | tee -a $OUTFILE
date | tee -a $OUTFILE

cd $SIMPL_HOME/bin
fclogger -n LOGGER > $TEST_DIR/results/junk &

cd $TEST_HOME/sudoku/bin
engine -n ENGINE -l LOGGER &
sleep 1

if [ -f $TEST_DIR/data/size16 ]
then
  SIZE=16
else
  SIZE=9
fi

python gui.py gui.py ENGINE  $SIZE

fcslay ENGINE
```

```
fcslay LOGGER

echo "Test finished you can run posttest $TEST_NO for result"
```

Note that the engine and gui.py executable files are pulled from the master Sudoku install area (sudoku/bin). This is standard practice for an integration test.[1]

There are several areas we would want to investigate using test sb004.

- We want to send the engine program the test puzzle just as we did in test sb002. The difference is that unlike the sim, the engine program will actually solve the puzzle and reply the solution.

- We would want to enter various Sudoku puzzles from any readily available Sudoku puzzle book. This will allow us to observe that the engine correctly solves the puzzles in a timely manner.

- We will want to deliberately send bad puzzle entries for submission to see if the puzzle engine reports an error.

- We will want to *play*, perhaps by creating some puzzles of our own. One way is to take the test puzzle and remove some of the values or change the values around. The results can be very surprising.

All of the script code associated with test sb004 is available in the accompanying tarball for the book.[2]

In any project of real world complexity, integration tests are by definition complex. This is not the optimal place to debug and solve a code defect. If an error is spotted in the behaviour of the engine or the Python GUI in the integration test phase, the better approach is to first try to replicate the error in the respective unit test (or a derivative of that unit test). It is more cost effective to spend the effort to replicate the error in a well defined unit test environment than in a more complex and less easily controlled integration test. Once the defect is isolated in this manner, the code is repaired and retested in the same unit test environment. Only once the defect fix is validated in the unit test is the repaired code rerun in the integration test to close off the sequence.

---

[1]The astute reader will recognize that in our simple project the master install area and the local build area are the same. This is not normally the case in more complex projects.

[2]If you wish to follow along with some real code in front of you the entire Sudoku project code is available at **http://www.icanprogram.com/simplBook**.

The STF and the decomposition of an application into SIMPL modules makes this type of testing sequence (unit-integration-defect-unit-integration) easier to manage.

16.1 Summary

In this chapter we discussed the integration test of the Python GUI with the Sudoku engine. If everything ran per spec, we have virtually completed this part of the project because the real world deployment would be very similar to the dotest script with the exception that the GUI and the engine would be run on different host computers.

Whatever other games are to be created, they would follow exactly the same development route that we have mapped out with Sudoku.

The SIMPL paradigm of modular design and the accompanying SIMPL testing framework make debugging complex software easier.

16.2 Next Chapter

In the next chapter we are going to look at what it would take to expand the Sudoku software along various lines such as networking and a Tcl/Tk GUI to arrive at the full feature set described in the original project spec.

Chapter 17

Sudoku Evolution

In Chapter 10 we discussed the system picture which would match the project specification. We also discussed the simplest possible subimplementation which had any value and we implemented that first, ie. the Sudoku GUI and puzzle processing engine. The testing framework was built for this simplified system and the code was written and tested. At this point we have working a Sudoku Python client and a working *single threaded* Sudoku puzzle engine.

In this chapter we are going to explore in various levels of detail, extending what we already have into a more practical system.

17.1   Forking Engine

One of the advantages of the SIMPL paradigm is that we can start with the basics and then methodically evolve that basic design to arrive at the more feature filled spec. In our case the next logical evolution for the Sudoku engine would be to give it the capability to handle simultaneous client connections. The tried and true approach to threading the engine is to have each new connection fork a child process and hand off the SIMPL channel to that child (see Figure 17.1.

The advantage of a forked engine over the single threaded engine is that each puzzle client will get its own instance of a puzzle engine. Multiple clients won't get held up if a particular puzzle takes time to solve. In a forked engine architecture, when the puzzle client has completed all of its requests for solutions to Sudoku puzzles, both the client and the forked engine instances will vanish.

A forked engine is still going to be a SIMPL receiver. Much of the previous algorithm will be retained intact. The only addition will be the algorithm for

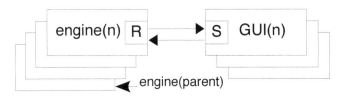

Figure 17.1: Forked Engine

forking a child process upon receiving a valid message token. While the forking SIMPL receiver will help with load balancing, it doesn't complete the evolution of our puzzle engine to conform with our original system picture. For that we need one more step to convert the forking SIMPL engine (receiver) into a forking SIMPL agent (sender). In Section 6.6 we saw that there is little difference between processing a SIMPL message which is captured via the **Receive** function and a SIMPL message captured by the **Reply** function. So flipping the engine around from a receiver to an agent involves little more than flipping a couple of SIMPL function calls. What does change radically however, is the blocking behaviour of the two variations. To see this best we need to examine the other half of the switch, the GUI. In our first pass the GUI was a SIMPL sender. In order to communicate with the agent the GUI needs to revert to becoming a SIMPL sender/receiver. Supposing we submitted a particularly difficult puzzle to our original engine. Since that version of the GUI used a blocking **Send** to communicate the puzzle we could notice a *freezing* of the GUI while the engine crunched away on the puzzle. Frozen GUI's are not good from the user's perspective. Our forking engine version would suffer from the same difficulty. However, if we send the puzzle to the agency and receive an immediate response, the GUI event loop is freed. Meanwhile the agency would hand the puzzle to the next available puzzle agent (a sender) who in turn would inform the GUI of the solution by utilizing the the GUI **Receive** port. The end result would be that no matter how long the engine took to solve a puzzle the GUI would remain responsive throughout.

If the reader is interested in the 'C' code that would be employed in making a forked engine, such code can be found in two of the TCP/IP surrogate program files: viz. surrogate_R.c and surrogate_S.c. These files accompany the main SIMPL tarball.

17.2   Networked Sudoku

Our project spec calls for a networked connection between the client GUI and
the server engine. Recalling Chapter 7 and relabelling Figure 7.1 we now have
Figure 17.2

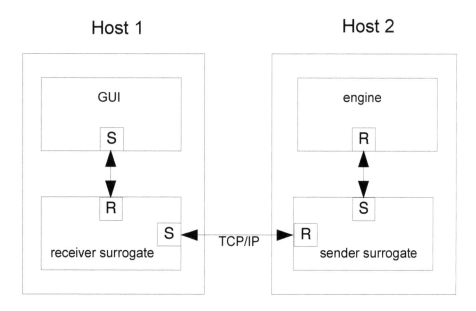

Figure 17.2: Networked Sudoku

We discuss TCP/IP surrogates because the TCP/IP network protocol is deployed widely. For convenience we will use two start up scripts, one for each
host. For simplicity we'll illustrate the networked Sudoku for our *simplest system which would work* initial design: a Python GUI (sender) and a 'C' engine
(receiver).

On host 1 where the GUI will be running, we have the following start up
script:

```
1  # startup  script  for  host  1
2
3  #!/bin/sh
4
5  export  FIFO_PATH=/home/fifo
6  export  SIMPL_PATH=/home/simpl
7
8  ./stopHost1
```

```
 9  sleep 1
10
11  echo starting protocolRouter
12  $SIMPL_PATH/bin/protocolRouter &
13  sleep 1
14
15  echo starting surrogateTcp
16  $SIMPL_PATH/bin/surrogateTcp &
17
18  echo ""
19  echo "==========================="
20  echo "1) 9x9 puzzle"
21  echo "2) 16x16 puzzle"
22  echo ""
23  echo -n "-> "
24  read ans
25
26  if [ $ans == '1' ]
27  then
28      SIZE=9
29  else
30      SIZE=16
31  fi
32
33  echo starting Python GUI
34  REMOTE_NAME="SIMPL_TCP:host2:ENGINE"
35  python gui.py gui.py $REMOTE_NAME $SIZE
```

line 3 Use the default system shell.

line 5 We export the FIFO_PATH shell variable that is required by SIMPL. Ordinarily, the FIFO_PATH would be exported at host boot up time via /etc/profile or equivalent.

line 6 We export the SIMPL_PATH shell variable SIMPL so that we can access the SIMPL surrogate and protocol router required by the script. Again, the SIMPL_PATH would also be exported at host boot up time via /etc/profile or equivalent.

line 8 We run a stop script which is in the same directory as this start script in order to shut down any possibly left over programs. The stop script is also available in the source code tarball.

line 12 We start the protocol router program required by the surrogate program in the background.

line 16 We start the surrogate which uses the TCP/IP protocol for remote communications.

lines 18-31 The script asks the user for the size of puzzle to be worked on (9x9 or 16x16).

line 34 **Important**: The SIMPL name of the remote engine program is set here. This is the means by which remote SIMPL communications are achieved. A local communication would merely state the SIMPL name of the receiving program or the the name of the common host and the SIMPL name of the receiving program. Notice that the name is composed of three parts which are delimited by colons. The first field is the protocol to be used, *SIMPL_TCP*. This field entry is actually unnecessary in our case because we have only one type of surrogate running. Nevertheless, it is more general and forces the programmer to be aware that the TCP/IP surrogate has been chosen as the mode of remote SIMPL communications. The second field, *host2*, is the host name of the computer where the Sudoku engine program is running and is naturally unique. Because this host name differs from the host name of the computer running this script, it is understood that remote communications will be required. The last field, *ENGINE*, is the SIMPL name of the Sudoku engine program.

line 35 The Python GUI program is started. The first field is the Python interpreter. It is assumed that there is a *PATH* to this executable. The second field, gui.py is the name of the Python GUI program. The third field is the SIMPL name of the Python GUI program. The fourth field is the SIMPL name of the remote Sudoku engine program. Finally, the fifth field indicates the size of the puzzle to be worked on.

On host 2 where the Sudoku engine will be running, we have the following start up script:

```
1  # startup  script  for  host 2
2
3  #!/bin/sh
4
5  export FIFO_PATH=/home/fifo
6  export SIMPL_PATH=/home/simpl
7
8  ./stopHost2
9  sleep 1
```

```
10
11  echo starting protocolRouter
12  $SIMPL_PATH/bin/protocolRouter &
13  sleep 1
14
15  echo starting surrogateTcp
16  $SIMPL_PATH/bin/surrogateTcp &
17
18  echo starting logger
19  $SIMPL_PATH/bin/fclogger -n LOGGER >./junk &
20
21  echo starting sudoku engine
22  ./engine -n ENGINE -l LOGGER &
```

Observe the symmetry between the host 1 and host 2 start up scripts.

line 3 Use the default system shell.

line 5 We export the FIFO_PATH shell variable that is required by SIMPL. Ordinarily, the FIFO_PATH would be exported at host boot up time via /etc/profile or equivalent.

line 6 We export the SIMPL_PATH shell variable SIMPL so that we can access the SIMPL surrogate and protocol router required by the script. Again, the SIMPL_PATH would also be exported at host boot up time via /etc/profile or equivalent.

line 8 We run a stop script which is in the same directory as this script in order to shut down any possibly left over programs. The stop script is also available in the source code tarball.

line 12 We start the protocol router program required by the surrogate program.

line 16 We start the surrogate which uses the TCP/IP protocol for remote communications.

line 19 The logger is started. It's a good place to start for debugging problems. Any problems/warnings/comments etc. will be written to the *junk* file in current directory. As well, don't forget to examine /var/tmp/simpl for warnings/errors relating to problems with SIMPL.

line 22 The Sudoku engine is started up. The SIMPL name of the engine and the name of the logger program follow on the command line.

The startup order is important for SIMPL. A receiver must have registered its SIMPL name before another process tries to connect to it. Hence the startup script for host 2 must be run before the startup script on host 1.[1]

These scripts are modelled after the integration test scripts (sb004) discussed in Chapter 16. The system should run indistinguishably from test sb004. If it does not, clues to problems associated with networked Sudoku will manifest in either the trace log or the main SIMPL log (/var/tmp/simpl on Linux). It is important to note that aside from starting up the relevant surrogate programs, the only difference between sb004 and the networked Sudoku is in the SIMPL name that the Python GUI (sender) uses to locate the Sudoku engine (receiver). On most SIMPl installations, the relevant surrogate and protocol router programs are started and backgrounded during system boot along with other Linux daemon processes.

17.3 Tcl/Tk GUI

In our original design we made provision for another GUI written in Tcl/Tk, mainly to allow access from non-Linux desktops. The Python GUI could do this in principle, but the required tclSurrogate protocol has so far only been implemented as a Tcl/Tk library.

The Tcl/Tk GUI unit test is broken into two separate tests: sb003 and sb003s depending on whether the shared guilib or the surrogate guilib is used. The shared guilib would be used for the Linux desktop and the surrogate guilib would be used for non-Linux desktop clients.

Let's focus on sb003 (see Figure 17.3) because the exercise will be the same for sb003s.

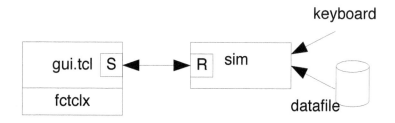

Figure 17.3: Tcl/Tk GUI unit tests sb003/sb003s

---

[1]A more complicated variation of these two scripts can be built to allow for retries to relax this sequencing requirement somewhat.

There are multiple aspects of the Tcl/Tk GUI that need to be validated. Most of those, such as verifying the *Save* and *Restore* functionality are entirely internal to the client code and don't involve any interaction with the puzzle engine. Test sb003 also concerns itself with unit testing the interaction between the client GUI and the sim. We want to verify the SIMPL message exchange between the client and the sim.

What follows is in part very similar to the Python/Tk unit test. The simulator (sim) in this test accesses a hard coded puzzle solution. The GUI contains a hard coded test puzzle which matches this. As such the primary test will consist of pressing the *Test* button in the GUI and verifying the solution that sim replies back to the GUI.

The engine protocol also contains provision for a PUZZLE_FAILURE token. The sim will respond with this token if any other puzzle than the canned one is submitted. We want to verify that the GUI responds by putting up a message dialog indicating a failure.

In order to perform our unit test for the Tcl/Tk GUI we run the following commands:

- dotest sb003

- posttest sb003

The pretest script for sb003 will not be needed because all the setup is preset in the GUI code itself and the Tcl/Tk script is only capable of sending 9x9 sized puzzles, unlike the Python/Tk GUI which can also send 16x16 sized puzzles.

The dotest script for sb003 would look something like the version below. Note that the sim and gui.tcl executable files are pulled from the local Sudoku build area. This is standard practice for a unit test.

```
#!/bin/bash

TEST_NO=sb003
TEST_DESC="Tcl/Tk gui unit test"

TEST_DIR=$TEST_HOME/testing/test$TEST_NO
OUTFILE=$TEST_DIR/results/test.out

echo "Starting up test #$TEST_NO" | tee $OUTFILE
echo $TEST_DESC | tee -a $OUTFILE
date | tee -a $OUTFILE

cd $SIMPL_HOME/bin
```

```
fclogger -n LOGGER > $TEST_DIR/results/junk &

cd $TEST_HOME/sudoku/bin
sim -n ENGINE -p $TEST_DIR/data -l LOGGER &

gui.tcl -N TCLGUI -R engine

fcslay ENGINE
fcslay LOGGER

echo "Test finished you can run posttest $TEST_NO for result"
```

When the *dotest sb003* is run a screen something like Figure 17.4 will come up on the test system (at least after the *Test* button is selected).

The idea is that this matches the canned puzzle in the sim (Sudoku engine stub) and if we submit this we expect to get back a valid solution to this puzzle. Since the puzzle solution will be rendered on the dotest GUI it will be necessary to run the posttest script (which contains the valid solution) from a separate console.

The engine protocol can also respond with a failure token. To stimulate this test case we repeat the pretest and dotest steps but rather than selecting the test puzzle we arbitrarily assign a couple of numbers in the blank puzzle and submit that. In this instance the sim is designed to respond with a failure token and we expect that the GUI will present a failure dialog.

All of the code associated with test sb003 is available in the accompanying tarball for the book.[2]

The bulk of the gui.tcl code relates to the widgets presented in the client window itself. These Tcl/Tk details are beyond the scope of this book. Suffice to say that the whole GUI client is contained in less than 350 lines (including white space) of Tcl/Tk script code.

---

[2]If you wish to follow along with some real code in front of you the entire Sudoku project code is available at **http://www.icanprogram.com/simplBook**.

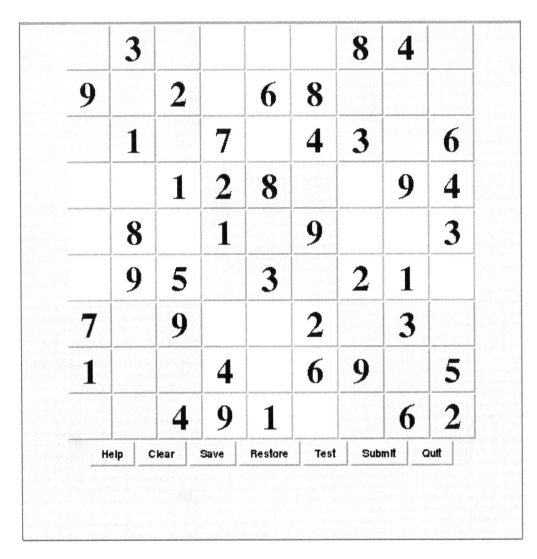

Figure 17.4: Tcl/Tk GUI screen

Of more interest to the reader are the SIMPL aspects of the Tcl/Tk GUI
script. If we examine the first few lines of the script we find:

```
#!/usr/bin/wish
#
# Tcl/Tk Sudoku Gui
# for SIMPL Book
#

set recvName ENGINE
```

```
set MYTOKEN(DO_9)        0

lappend auto_path $env(SIMPL_HOME)/lib
source ./guilib.tcl
```

In the *recvName* variable we are stuffing the default SIMPL name for the sim (a SIMPL receiver). This name will subsequently be used in a **name_locate** call. We also see the 9x9 puzzle token being captured as a Tcl/Tk array element.

The most important element in this code block is the line which includes the guilib.tcl code. This is the only code which differs between the Linux desktop (shared library) version of our script and the other desktop (surrogate library) version of our script. With the use of Makefile magic we simply arrange to have different lines of code get absorbed into the script depending on our intended desktop. It is worth examining these two variations in more detail. They are contained as the guilib.shared and the guilib.surrogate source files respectively. The contents of guilib.shared are listed below:

```
package require Fctclx
```

Fctclx is the name of the Tcl/Tk SIMPL shared library which extends the SIMPL command set to include all of the basic SIMPL API. viz. **Send**, **Receive**, **Reply** etc. The guilib.surrogate file is only marginally more complex as shown below:

```
set gatewayAddr 127.0.0.1
set gatewayPort 8000
package require fcgateway
package require fcsocket
```

Here we need to specify two global variables for the IP address (or URL) and the port number associated with the tclSurrogate partner used to enable transparent SIMPL communications with non-Linux platforms.[3] The fcgateway and the fcsocket are Tcl/Tk packages (libraries) which encapsulate the tclSurrogate protocol (fcsocket) and then abstract this as the SIMPL Send/Receive/Reply API (fcgateway). See Appendix E.[4]

The next SIMPL aspect in our GUI script of note is the section at the bottom which concerns itself with the SIMPL **name_attach** and **name_locate** setup. This is illustrated in the following code snip:

---

[3]The sample guilib.surrogate listing shows the loopback address (127.0.0.1) for the gatewayAddr and the default tclSurrogate port (8000) for the gatewayPort.

[4]fcgateway and fcsocket are part of the SIMPL-Tcl/Tk tarball which can be downloaded and installed according to A.6

```
set fn main
wm geometry .  600x600+200+0
wm title .  "SIMPL Book Tcl/Tk Sudoku Gui"
wm resizable . 0 0

set myName TCLGUI

set state flag
foreach arg $argv {
  switch -- $state {
    flag {
      switch -glob -- $arg {
        -N { set state name }
        -R { set state recv }
        -P { set state port }
        -G { set state gateway }
        default { error "unknown flag $arg"}
      }
    }

    name {
      set myName $arg
      set state flag
    }

    recv {
      set recvName $arg
      set state flag
    }

    port {
      set gatewayPort $arg
      set state flag
    }

    gateway {
      set gatewayAddr $arg
      set state flag
    }
  };# end switch state
};# end foreach

name_attach $myName

set recvID [name_locate $recvName]
```

The first part of this logic concerns itself with the capture of command line parameter options associated with gui.tcl. These include things like the -N parameter for overriding the default SIMPL name given to gui.tcl or the -R option for overriding the default SIMPL name for the puzzle engine (sim in this instance) discussed in Chapter 13. This logic is immediately followed by two standard SIMPL code lines for attaching the SIMPL name to the client process and then opening the SIMPL channel to the puzzle solving engine.

There is a ***name_detach*** section at the end of script which gets executed as a result of selecting the *Quit* button.

```
button $br.quit −text Quit −command {set x 1}
pack $br.quit −side left

pack $br −side bottom
pack $f

vwait x

name_detach

exit
```

The vwait command in Tcl waits on a change in a variable while continuing to execute the Tk event loop. When we select *Quit* we change this monitored variable which sends the script to the exit and passing the ***name_detach*** call en route.

The final SIMPL code block of interest is contained in the hndlSubmit procedure reproduced below:

```
#================================================
# hndlSubmit − entry point
#================================================
proc hndlSubmit {} {
global recvID
global MYTOKEN
global puzzle

hndlSave

set elements ""
for {set r 0} {$r < 9} {incr r} {
  for {set c 0} {$c < 9} {incr c} {
    set elements [format "%s%s" $elements $puzzle(.f.$r.$c)]
  };# end for c
};#end for r
```

```
set rc -1
if {$recvID != -1} {
  set sMsg [binary format "i1a*" \
    $MYTOKEN(DO_9)\
    $elements]

  set sBytes [string length $sMsg]
  set rMsg [Send $recvID $sMsg $sBytes]

  binary scan $rMsg i1i1i1a* slot rbytes token rpuzzle

  if {$token != $MYTOKEN(DO_9) } {
    tk_messageBox -message [format "puzzle error"]
  } else {

  set i 0
  for {set r 0} {$r < 9} {incr r} {
    for {set c 0} {$c < 9} {incr c} {
    set puzzle(.f.$r.$c) [string index $rpuzzle $i]
    incr i
    };#end for c
  };# end for r
  set rc 1
  };# end else token
  };# end if recvID

return $rc
};# end hndlSubmit
```

One can easily spot the SIMPL **Send** command and its tokenized message setup preamble including the assignment of the token for a 9x9 puzzle. The binary scan command which follows is decoding the reply which comes back from the puzzle engine. The Tcl/Tk libraries prepend some header information (slot, rbytes) to the actual SIMPL message.

The rest of the gui.tcl script concerns itself with widget manipulation to provide the balance of the functionality in our Sudoku puzzle client.

17.4 Summary

In this chapter we have discussed extending our locally run Sudoku client/server by:

1. Adding a forking engine capability.

2. Networking the client GUI with the server engine.

3. Adding a Tcl/Tk GUI.

In our original spec we defined other possible word puzzles. Completing this ambitious spec is beyond the scope of this book. Suffice to say that those other puzzle engines would be developed along the same lines as the Sudoku program. What is important is that we've used Sudoku to illustrate SIMPL and the SIMPL approach to problem solving. Despite the fact that our spec was rather *concocted*, hopefully the reader is left with the impression that SIMPL can be used to systematically approach a complicated real world spec.

Chapter 18

Conclusion

When we were first exposed to the Send/Receive/Reply messaging we found it to be an immensely powerful way to create software. As we got more involved we found that this messaging approach encouraged us to decompose our problems into manageable modules. As we worked on more diverse projects of real world complexity we found that our repository of seed code grew steadily. We believe that Kevin Kelly got it right when he said that complex systems are best grown from simple systems which already work.[1]

As our SIMPL repository grew we recognized that we had repeating patterns in our solutions. We coined the term softwareIC to encapsulate this observation. Like the hardware IC did for the hardware designer, we believe the softwareIC will lower project risk, cost and time to market for the software designer. We have found that SIMPL is a great tool for creating softwareICs.

We also found (through trial and error) that our testing framework helps lower the risks associated with a complex project. We like the fact that with SIMPL we can build our modules and test them locally, confident that with the use of surrogates they will *simply work* when deployed across a network. When it comes to programming languages, we are pragmatic and we like the fact that the SIMPL toolkit allows us to create SIMPL modules in 'C', Tcl/Tk, and Python at this time. In future, perhaps the SIMPL library will be extended to other languages and formats.

It is no accident that when searching for acronyms for the nascent project that we settled on SIMPL. The KISS (Keep it Simple Stupid) principle is central to our programming philosophy and its influence pervades the SIMPL toolkit. Many useful SIMPL applications can be written using only the core five functions

---

[1]Out of Control: The New Biology of Machines, Social Systems, and the Economic World by Kevin Kelly, Addison-Wesley Pub., 1994, ISBN 0-210-48340-8

in the SIMPL library, viz. *name_attach, name_locate, Send, Receive, Reply*.

We have found that a project specification is a moving target more often than not. As such, it is almost always best to start with the simplest possible subset of features that target users will find useful and code them first. It is always best to engage the users as early as possible in exercising this code. We do this with the confidence that our tokenized message enabled SIMPL modules will allow us to evolve our feature sets in unison with the user's wishes.

We built the SIMPL toolkit because we found it useful. We released the SIMPL toolkit as open source because we think you'll find it useful as well. We acknowledge the contributions of many other programmers who have donated their efforts into the open source pool. As a result, the barrier to entry for a new Linux programmer is as low as it gets. The SIMPL toolkit truly stands on the contributions of many.

Finally, we wrote this book because it was time. It was time to collect our experience and make it available to a new generation of Linux developers; we hope that you will find it helpful.

Part V

Appendices

Appendix A

Installation

A.1 Installing SIMPL Core Code

Before you begin you will need to make a couple of decisions about where your SIMPL source tree will exist and where your SIMPL sandbox will exist. The locations of these two areas are governed by a couple of environment variables that you need to set.

- SIMPL_HOME - locates the source tree (must end with *simpl*). For example: */home/simpl*

- FIFO_PATH - locates the SIMPL sandbox. For example: */home/fifo*

The SIMPL_HOME environment variable is only used by the SIMPL build scripts and Makefiles. The FIFO_PATH environment variable is used internally by the SIMPL library to execute ***name_attach*** and ***name_locate*** calls.

The SIMPL source tree has been carefully designed not to *pollute* your system. All SIMPL related files will exist under one of these two directories above.

You are now ready to go on line and grab the latest version of SIMPL source code from the SIMPL Open Source project website:

> *http://www.icanprogram.com/simpl*

or the Sourceforge repository for SIMPL at:

> *https://sourceforge.net/projects/simpl*

The SIMPL project is a dynamic Open Source project and releases are made regularly. It is also quite stable.

It is important that you pick up the latest release to capture all the bug fixes that have been done. When in doubt which version to use, the Sourceforge site always contains the latest release.

Once you have downloaded the latest tarball you need to place it at the subdirectory immediately above the SIMPL_HOME directory. ie.

```
cd $SIMPL_HOME
cd ..
<place your SIMPL tarball here>
```

You can undo your tarball by typing:

```
tar -zxvf whateveryourSIMPLtarballnameis.tar.gz
```

At this point you should have a whole bunch of source code sitting at SIMPL_HOME.

On a Linux system for example, SIMPL_HOME and FIFO_PATH are usually exported during system boot via /etc/profile as follows:


```
export FIFO_PATH=/home/fifo
export SIMPL_HOME=/home/simpl
```

The actual directory locations can of course be anything you want them to be.

A.2   Building the SIMPL Core Libraries

After installing all the source on your system the next step is to build all this source code into the SIMPL libraries. To do this you will need to:

```
cd $SIMPL_HOME/scripts
./buildsimpl
```

This should cause the SIMPL source to completely build and install itself. For errors you can examine the $SIMPL_HOME/make.out file that this script produces.

Being a library, it is not immediately obvious that SIMPL is operational. One of the subdirectories under the SIMPL_HOME tree is called **benchmarks**. Some SIMPL executables were built here. They can be used to *time* the SIMPL message passing on your system. We will be using them here to verify that you have SIMPL installed and the environment variables are correctly defined. The buildsimpl script should have caused two executables to be built. Namely,

- $SIMPL_HOME/benchmarks/bin/receiver

- $SIMPL_HOME/benchmarks/bin/sender

To run this benchmark test you will need to open two text consoles on your system and point each to the $SIMPL_HOME/benchmarks/bin directory.

On console 1, logged onto $SIMPL_HOME/benchmarks/bin type:

```
receiver -n BOBR
```

where BOBR - is an arbitrary SIMPL name you have chosen for this receiver. On console 2, logged onto $SIMPL_HOME/benchmarks/bin type:

```
sender -n BOBS -r BOBR -t 100000 -s 1024
```

where

- -n BOBS - is the SIMPL name for the sender.

- -r BOBR - is the SIMPL name used for the receiver.

- -t 100000 - send 100000 messages before displaying timing.

- -s 1024 - makes each message 1024 bytes in length (same size for replies).

When you hit enter on console 2 the sender locates the receiver and then marks the time. It then procedes to send 100000 1k messages to the receiver, each time blocking for the same size reply.

If you see segment faults in the above this is a clear indication that you do not have your FIFO_PATH environment variable defined in such a way that they are set for each login.

When this preset number of messages has been exchanged the sender calculates and reports the total elapsed time in msec.

You have asked your system to do a substantial piece of work here. Depending on your processor type and speed this may take several tens of seconds to complete. Once you have the number you can easily compute the number of SIMPL messages per second that your system is capable of exchanging.

At this point you will have successfully installed the core SIMPL libraries.

A.3 SIMPL Public SoftwareICs Code Repository

We discussed the concept of softwareICs at length in the book. The SIMPL project maintains a public repository of several softwareICs. These can be used as seed code for starting any project.

Step 1: To obtain the latest softwareICs tarball you'll need to visit the main SIMPL project website at: *http://www.icanprogram.com/simpl*

Step 2: Locate and download the softwareICs tarball and place it one level above the $SIMPL_HOME directory.

```
cd $SIMPL_HOME
cd ..
<place softwareICs tarball here>
```

Step 3: Undo that tarball to install the softwareICs code.

```
tar -zxvf simplics.tar.gz
```

Step 4: You can now build the softwareICs code by going to the top level area and running the top level make at that location.

```
cd $SIMPL_HOME/softwareICs
make clobber
make install
```

This will create a series of executables at $SIMPL_HOME/softwareICs/bin.

Step 5: Each softwareIC test subdirectory will contain a README file describing how that code can be executed. While this is of immense value in understanding how each of these pieces work, the real value of this software repository is as seed code for any SIMPL project you tackle.

A.4 SIMPL Testing Framework

The SIMPL testing framework was discussed at length in Chapter 8.

Step 1: On the main SIMPL website you find the SIMPL testing framework tarball. Download and install that as you have done before.

```
cd $SIMPL_HOME
cd ..
<place simpltest.tar.gz here>
```

Step 2: Undo the tarball to expose the SIMPL framework wrapper scripts.

```
tar -zxvf simpltest.tar.gz
```

This will create an $SIMPL_HOME/testing tree and place all of the existing SIMPL test scripts there. It will also populate the $SIMPL_HOME/scripts area with the SIMPL testing framework wrapper scripts.

Step 3: Setup the framework.

You'll need to create an environment variable called TEST_HOME which will point at your particular project. For now just point this TEST_HOME at $SIMPL_HOME

```
export TEST_HOME=$SIMPL_HOME
```

If the $SIMPL_HOME/scripts is in your PATH you can simply type:

```
seetest i
```

If you see a list of the SIMPL tests, your installation has been successful.

A.5   Python SIMPL

SIMPL also comes with source for a Python SIMPL library. This source is composed of 'C' wrappers which are used to create a Python SIMPL module thereby *extending* Python's capabilities.

It will be necessary for you to have the following items available on your system in order to run Python SIMPL:

1. The Python interpreter *python*. On a Linux system you may find out whether the interpreter is present by typing *which python* at the command line. If you don't get something like */usr/bin/python*, then either the interpreter is not within your command path or it is not present. In the former case you will have to export the directory location to your command path and in the latter case you will have to obtain a copy of the interpreter.

2. The Python 'C' library and headers. On a Linux system you will likely find the necessary files under */usr/include/python2.5* and */usr/lib/python2.5* or under */usr/share*. The 2.5 suffix is an example of a Python version number. Without these files the Python SIMPL module cannot be made.

If you have gotten this far, then all of the above files are present and available on your system; now you have to obtain the SIMPL software.

Step 1: From the main SIMPL website download the Python hooks SIMPL tarball onto your system.

Step 2: To undo the tarball by perform the following steps:

```
cd $SIMPL_HOME
cd .. (yes that's up one level from $SIMPL_HOME)
<place the simplpython.tar.gz here>
tar -zxvf simplpython.tar.gz
```

This will create an $SIMPL_HOME/python tree and place all of the source for the code in there.

Step 3: Build the code.

This is where most novice SIMPL users have difficulty. The SIMPL Python code is used to create amongst other things a shared library in the form of a module which renders the SIMPL API as Python functions. In order to successfully compile this module your compiler must have access to the Python source headers and library as was discussed above in the necessary items list. So if your Linux distribution doesn't have those installed you'll need to do that first before proceeding.

If the $SIMPL_HOME/scripts is in your command PATH you can simply type:

```
buildsimpl.python
```

Alternatively you can,

```
cd $SIMPL_HOME/python
make clobber
make install
```

This will create the Python module and move it to $SIMPL_HOME/modules.

Step 4: Run the examples. There are some examples of Python SIMPL code in the $SIMPL_HOME/python/test directory as well as in the *http://www.icanprogram.com/simpl/eg_installation.html* examples tarball.

A.6 Tcl SIMPL

The SIMPL toolkit comes with hooks for the Tcl language. These hooks let you create SIMPL modules using the Tcl scripting language.

It will be necessary for you to have the following items available on your system in order to run Tcl SIMPL:

1. The Tcl interpreter *wish*. On a Linux system you may find out whether it is present by typing *which wish* at the command line. If you don't get something like */usr/bin/wish* then either the interpreter is not within your command path or it is not present. In the former case you will have to export the directory location to your command path and in the latter case you will have to obtain a copy of the interpreter.

2. The Tcl 'C' library and headers. On a Linux system you will likely find the necessary files under */usr/include/tcl8.4* and */usr/lib/tcl8.4* or under */usr/share*. The 8.4 suffix is the version number. Without these files the Tcl SIMPL module cannot be made.

If you have gotten this far, then all of the above files are present and available on your system; now you have to obtain the SIMPL software.

Step 1: From the main SIMPL website download the Tcl tarball.

Step 2: To undo the tarball by perform the following steps:

```
cd $SIMPL_HOME
cd .. (yes that's up one level from $SIMPL_HOME)
<place the simpltcl.tar.gz here>
tar -zxvf simpltcl.tar.gz
```

This will create an $SIMPL_HOME/tcl tree and place all of the source for the code in there.

Step 3: Build the code.

This is where most novice SIMPL users have difficulty. The SIMPL Tcl code is used to create amongst other things a shared library which exposes the SIMPL API as Tcl commands. In order to successfully compile this shared library your compiler must have access to the Tcl source headers as was described above in the necessary items list. So if your Linux distribution doesn't have those installed you'll need to do that first before proceding.

If the $SIMPL_HOME/scripts is in your command PATH you can simply type:

```
buildsimpl.tcl
```

Alternatively you can,

```
cd $SIMPL_HOME/tcl
make clobber
make install
```

This will create the Tcl shared library and move it to $SIMPL_HOME/lib.

Step 4: Run the examples. There are some examples of Tcl SIMPL code in the $SIMPL_HOME/tcl/test directory as well as in the emphhttp://www.icanprogram.com/simpl/eg_installation.html examples tarball.

Appendix B

Library Functions

The following sections contain descriptions of the SIMPL library calls offered at the time of printing.

B.1 'C' Language Functions

int name_attach(char *processName, void (*exitFunc)())

Description: The name_attach() function is required by every process that expects to send/receive messages to/from any other process. It is responsible for setting up all of the SIMPL functionality that may be required. It must precede any other SIMPL library calls. The string processName is the desired SIMPL name of the process. This name must be unique on each host but not necessarily on a network. A process that has successfully called this function is often referred to as being *name attached*. The length of processName is defined as follows:

$$0 < length \leq \text{MAX\_PROGRAM\_NAME\_LEN}$$

If the name is too large it is truncated to MAX_PROGRAM_NAME_LEN to fit. The exitFunc() is some function that the programmer wants to have run when the process exits or in the case of the occurrence of a SIGTERM or similar signal (ie. one that can be trapped). It returns 0 for success and -1 for failure. Failures may occur due to:

1. The name string processName is too short (zero bytes).

2. The environment variable FIFO_PATH has not been defined.

3. processName is not unique on that particular host.

4. A receive FIFO could not be made.

5. A reply FIFO could not be made.

Example: The calling process wants to attach the SIMPL name "receiver".

```
#include <simpl.h>

void main()
{
int id;

// SIMPL name attach
id = name_attach("receiver");
if (id == -1)
  {
  printf("name attach error=%s\n", whatsMyError());
  exit(-1);
  }
}
```

int name_detach(void)

Description: The name_detach() function removes SIMPL related components from a program that has previously run a successful name_attach(). This call is made automatically by the atexit() procedure within SIMPL if the program itself doesn't call it directly; so in some ways it could be considered redundant. However, it is recommended if only for good form. It returns 0 on success or -1 on failure. Failure occurs if the calling process had never been name attached.

Example: The following process has successfully name attached SIMPL name "receiver" and either wants to detach the SIMPL functionality or it is terminating.

```
#include <simpl.h>

void main()
{
int id;

// SIMPL name attach
```

```
id = name_attach("receiver");
/*
  body of program
*/
// SIMPL name detach
name_detach();
}
```

int child_detach(void)

Description: The child_detach() function allows the child process of a forked parent to remove the common SIMPL components that exist in the parent and child processes after forking. This occurs if the parent has been name attached prior to the fork() call. The child_detach() call should be made prior to the child process running its own name_attach() if called. It returns 0 for success and -1 for failure. Failure occurs if the parent process was not name attached in the first place.

Example: The following name attached parent process has successfully forked a child process.

```
#include <simpl.h>

// parent process
void main()
{
int id;
pid_t pid;

// SIMPL name attach
id = name_attach("parent");

// fork child
pid = fork();
if (pid < 0) // fork failure
  {
  printf("fork error-%s\n", fn, strerror(errno));
  }
else if (pid == 0) // child
  {
  myChild();
  }
else // parent
  {
```

```
   /*
      body of program
   */
   }
}

// child process
void myChild()
{
int id;

// detach from parent's SIMPL components
child_detach();

// SIMPL name attach the child separately
id = name_attach("child");
/*
    body of program
*/
}
```

---

int sur_detach(int id)

Description: The sur_detach() function must be called if a process exits after running a successful name_locate() call for another process on a remote host. The sur_detach() will cause the surrogates to terminate by sending them SUR_CLOSE messages. The number of receiver surrogates is stored in a table internal to the sending process. Under normal circumstances this will be called internally by the name_detach() function in the case of process termination. The id passed into the function is the surrogate receiver FIFO id. This function is called as part of the atexit() function for any process that performs a non-local name_locate(). It returns 0 for success and -1 for failure. Failures may occur due to:

1. The id passed in is non-sequitor.

2. Communication errors with the receiver surrogate.

Example: The process name locates another process called "receiver" on remote host 192.168.1.42 via the RS-232 serial protocol. Later, it breaks the connection made by the name locate call.

```
#include <simpl.h>

void main()
{
int id;

// try to make a remote SIMPL connection
id = name_locate("SIMPL_RS232:192.168.1.42:receiver");
/*
    processing ...
*/
// remote connection no longer needed
sur_detach(id);
/*
    processing ...
*/
}
```

---

int name_locate(char *protocolName:hostName:processName)

Description: The name_locate() function must be called prior to a Send() or Trigger() call so that the sender may connect to the receiver it wishes to send to. The protocolName determines the ensuing remote protocol method of data exchange. If this is not set then a default is chosen. The default will be the first available protocol found in the protocol router's table. The hostName is the name of the host that the sender wishes to send to. It may be either a real host name (canonical or alias) or non-existent in the case of a local send. It can also be in the dotted network format. If the local host name/ip is used then SIMPL will run locally. The processName is the name of the receiving process that is name attached on that particular host. It returns the id of the receiver process that a message is to be sent to ≥ 0 or -1 for failure. Failures may occur due to:

1. The calling process was never name attached.

2. The protocol name is not supported.

3. The process name is NULL.

4. The HOSTNAME environment variable is not set.

5. Too many colons in the argument (maximum of 2).

And for remote name locates only:

6. Failure to contact the protocolRouter program.

7. No surrogates available.

8. Failure to contact remote surrogate.

9. Failure to find remote receiving program.

Example One: This is an example of where the name of the process of interest is running on the local host.

```
#include <simpl.h>

void main()
{
int id;

// no host name implies local host ==> local connection
id = name_locate("localProcessName");
/*
    processing ...
*/
}
```

OR

```
#include <simpl.h>

void main()
{
int id;

// host name is the local host ==> local connection
id = name_locate("localHostName:localProcessName");
/*
    processing ...
*/
}
```

Example Two: This is an example of where the process of interest is running on a remote host.

```
#include <simpl.h>

void main()
```

```
{
int id;

// default protocol, remote host name ==> remote connection
id = name_locate("remoteHostName:remoteProcessName");
/*
    processing ...
*/
}
```

OR

```
#include <simpl.h>

void main()
{
int id;

// specified protocol, remote host name ==> remote connection
id = name_locate("protocolName:remoteHostName:remoteProcessName");
/*
    processing ...
*/
}
```

Example Three: This process specifies the protocol type as SIMPL_TCP, the ip address 192.168.1.101 of the host and the receiver's SIMPL name is receiver1. If the ip address is the same as that of the local host then the communication will be local SIMPL and the protocol field will be ignored.

```
#include <simpl.h>

void main()
{
int id;

// specified protocol and dotted network name ==> remote connection
id = name_locate("SIMPL_TCP:192.168.1.101:receiver1");
/*
    processing ...
*/
}
```

---

int Receive(char **ptr, void *inArea, unsigned maxBytes)

Description: The Receive() function receives messages from senders in a memory area pointed to by inArea and no larger than that specified by maxBytes. In the case that inArea is NULL the maxBytes is ignored and the actual copying of the message can then be done via the simplRcopy() call. In this way an undetermined amount of memory can be accounted for by using dynamic allocation as opposed to some global or stack buffer if desired. The *ptr is set in the Receive() and uniquely identifies the sender. This value is later used for replies. This function returns a value of ≥ 0 for the size of an incoming message or $\leq$ -2 which indicates a proxy has been received or -1 for a failure. In the case of a proxy being sent you must call the function returnProxy(int ret) to obtain the true value of the proxy where ret is the Receive() return value. Failures can arise from:

1. The calling process was never name attached.

2. FIFO trigger problems.

3. Shared memory (shmem) problems.

Example One: This process is receiving a message with a size in bytes that is well known.

```
#include <simpl.h>

void main()
{
int msgSize;
char *sender;
char inArea[1024];
int maxBytes = 1024;

// SIMPL name attach
name_attach("receiver");
// receive messages
msgSize = Receive(&sender, inArea, maxBytes);
/*
    process message ...
*/
}
```

Example Two: This process is receiving a message with a size in bytes that is not well known.

```
#include <simpl.h>

void main()
{
int msgSize;
char *sender;
char *inArea;

// SIMPL name attach
name_attach("receiver");
// receive messages
msgSize = Receive(&sender, NULL, 0);
// dynamically allocate sufficient memory
inArea = malloc(msgSize);
// copy the message into the allocated memory
simplRcopy(sender, inArea, msgSize);
/*
    process message ...
*/
}
```

Example Three: This process is receiving a proxy.

```
#include <simpl.h>

void main()
{
int proxy;
int msgSize;
char *sender;
char inArea[1024];
int maxBytes = 1024;

// SIMPL name attach
name_attach("receiver");
// receive messages
msgSize = Receive(&sender, inArea, maxBytes);
if (msgSize < -1)
  {
  proxy = returnProxy(msgSize);
  }
/*
    react to proxy ...
*/
// a Reply() is unnecessary for a proxy
}
```

---

int Send(int id, void *out, void *in, unsigned outSize, unsigned inSize)

Description: The Send() function is a blocked send. This means that the calling program expects a reply from the receiver and waits until it gets one. The id is the result of a prior call to name_locate() with regard to the receiver of interest. The function sends a message to the receiver pointed to by out with message size = outSize in bytes. It expects a reply message from the receiver to be placed in memory pointed to by in with a size no larger than inSize in bytes. The function returns the size of the reply message ≥ 0 in bytes for success and -1 for a failure. Failures can occur due to:

1. The calling process was never name attached.

2. name_locate() was not run prior to the Send call.

3. FIFO problems.

4. Reply errors.

5. Reply message larger than inSize.

Example One: This process is sending to another local process called 'receiver' and is not expecting any return message.

```
#include <simpl.h>

void main()
{
int receiverId;
char outArea[1024];
int outBytes = 1024;

// SIMPL name attach
name_attach("sender");
// make connection
receiverId = name_locate{"receiver");
// send message to receiver expecting nothing in reply
Send(receiverId, outArea, outBytes; NULL, 0);
/*
   await null reply message from receiver ...
*/
}
```

Example Two: This process is sending to another local process called 'receiver' and is expecting any return message.

```c
#include <simpl.h>

void main()
{
int receiverId;
char outArea[1024];
char inArea[1024];
int inBytes = 100;
int outBytes = 512;

// SIMPL name attach
name_attach("sender");
// make connection
receiverId = name_locate{"receiver");
// send a mesage to receiver expecting a reply no larger than inBytes
Send(receiverId, outArea, outBytes, inArea, inBytes);
/*
    await and process reply message from receiver ...
*/
}
```

int Reply(char *ptr, void *outArea, unsigned size)

Description: The Reply() function responds a return message from a receiver to a blocked sender indicated by ptr. The reply message is pointed to by outArea and is of size in bytes. The function returns 0 for success and -1 for failure. Failures can occur due to:

1. The calling process was never name attached.

2. FIFO errors.

Example One: This process has received a message from 'sender' and is replying a null response because the sender is not expecting any return reply message.

```c
#include <simpl.h>

void main()
{
int msgSize;
char *sender;
char inArea[1024];
```

```
int maxBytes = 1024;

// SIMPL name attach
name_attach("receiver");
// receive messages
msgSize = Receive(&sender,inArea, maxBytes);
// reply null message
Reply(sender, NULL, 0);
/*
    process message ...
*/
}
```

Example Two: This process has received a message from 'sender' and is replying some sort of response.

```
#include <simpl.h>

void main()
{
int msgSize;
char *sender;
char inArea[1024];
char *outArea[1024];
int maxBytes = 1024;

// SIMPL name attach
name_attach("receiver");
// receive messages
msgSize = Receive(&sender,inArea, maxBytes);
/*
  process message and construct reply message...
*/
// reply message back to sender
Reply(sender, outArea, 1024);
}
```

int Trigger(int id, int proxy)

Description: The Trigger() function sends a proxy identified as an int to a receiving process identified by a prior call to name_locate() giving id. It is important that the proxy *MUST* be an integer > 0 AND < 7FFFFFFF. This can thought of as a kick to the receiver and requires no reply. This function returns 0 on success and -1 for a failure. Failures can occur due to:

1. The calling process was never name attached.

2. Receiver does not exist.

3. FIFO errors.

4. Proxy number is out of range.

Example: This process is triggering another local process called 'receiver'.

```
#include <simpl.h>

void main()
{
int proxy = 10;
int receiverId;

// SIMPL name attach
name_attach("sender");
// make connection to receiver
receiverId = name_locate{"receiver");
// send a proxy to receiver
Trigger(receiverId, proxy);
}
```

char *whatsMyName(void)

Description: The whatsMyName() function gets the SIMPL name of the calling process. It returns the SIMPL name on success and NULL on failure. Failure can occur if the calling process was never name attached.

Example: This process name attached itself as 'sender'. The result of the printf should be 'sender'.

```
#include <simpl.h>

void main()
{
// SIMPL name attach
name_attach("sender");

// print my SIMPL name
printf("My SIMPL name is %s\n", whatsMyName());
}
```

int whatsMyRecvfd(void)

Description: The whatsMyRecvfd() function gets the receive FIFO file descriptor of the calling process. If one has not been assigned, one will be made. The function returns the receive FIFO file descriptor on success and -1 on failure. Failures can occur due to:

1. The calling process was never name attached.

2. The FIFO could not be opened for read/write.

Example: This process name attached itself as 'sender'. The result of the whatsMyRecvfd() should be a file descriptor to its SIMPL receive FIFO. In this example we are allowing the process to 'kick' on either an incoming SIMPL message or a timer.

```
#include <simpl.h>

void main()
{
int ret;
int fd;
fd_set watchset;
fd_set inset;
struct timeval tv;
struct timeval *timeoutPtr;

// SIMPL name attach
name_attach("sender");

// get receive FIFO file descriptor
fd = whatsMyRecvfd();

// set select parameters
FD_ZERO(&watchset);
FD_SET(fds[0], &watchset);

// set timer parameters
tv.tv_sec = 10;
tv.tv_usec = 0;
timeoutPtr = &tv;

// let select kick on the file descriptor or the timer
```

```
ret = select(fd + 1, &watchset, NULL, NULL, timeoutPtr);
/*
       react on select ...
*/
}
```

int whatsMyReplyfd(void)

Description: The whatsMyReplyfd() function finds the reply FIFO file descriptor of the calling process. If one has not been assigned, one will be made. The function returns the reply FIFO file descriptor on success and -1 on failure. Failures can occur due to:

1. The calling process was never name attached.

2. The FIFO could not be opened for read/write.

Example: See the example in whatsMyRecvfd() and simply substitute the whatsMyReplyfd() call for the whatsMyRecvfd() call.

char *whatsMyError(void)

Description: The whatsMyError() function returns a descriptive string based on the last value of _simpl_errno. This is analogous to the well known errno/strerror(errno) combination in 'C'. The function returns a pointer to a the error string.

Example: See the example in name_attach().

void simplRcopy(char *src, void *dst, unsigned size)

Description: The simplRcopy() function copies size bytes from the memory pointed to by src to dst. It works in conjunction with a Receive(&id, NULL, 0) type call in order to extract the message data after the size of the message is known. The function returns nothing.

Example: See Example Two in Receive().

---

void simplScopy(void *dst, unsigned size)

Description: The simplScopy() copies size bytes from the memory pointed to by a sender's shmem pointer to dst. It works in conjunction with a Send(fd, &buf, NULL, outSize, inSize) call in order to extract the reply message data after the message is known. Note that inSize must be set to some maximal amount or internal checking will reject the transaction. The function returns nothing.

Example: This process is sending to another local process called 'receiver' but does not know how much memory to allocate for the reply message.

```
#include <simpl.h>

void main()
{
int receiverId;
char outArea[100];
int outSize = 100;
int inSize;
char *inArea;

// SIMPL name attach
name_attach("sender");
// make connection
receiverId = name_locate{"receiver");
// send a message to the receiver expecting nothing in reply
inSize = Send(receiverId, outArea, outSize; NULL, 0);
// dynamically allocate adequate memory for the reply message
inArea = malloc(inSize);
// now copy the message
simplScopy(inArea, inSize);
/*
      process the reply
*/
}
```

---

int simplReplySize(char *ptr)

Description: The simplReplySize() function reports the maximum size of the reply message expected by a sender. It is called between Receive() and Reply() calls. It returns the size of the expected reply message which is ≥ 0.

Example: This process receives a message from "sender" and then checks the maximum size of the expected reply.

```
#include <simpl.h>

void main()
{
int nBytes;
int yBytes;
char *sender;
char inArea[1024];

// receive message from the local sender
nBytes = Receive(&sender, inArea, 1024);
if (nBytes == -1)
  {
  printf("receive error-%s\n", whatsMyError());
  exit(-1);
  }

// what is the maximum size of the expected reply message?
yBytes = simplReplySize(sender);
/*
    processing ...
*/
}
```

void simplSetSenderParms(char *sender, SIMPL_REC *rec)

Description: The simplSetSenderParms() function stores the relevant SIMPL information with respect to "sender" in the structure "rec". This information can later be used to check on "sender's" veracity.

Example: This process receives a message from "sender" and later checks to see whether "sender" is still a valid SIMPL process.

```
#include <simpl.h>

void main()
{
int nBytes;
SIMPL_REC senderInfo;
char *sender;
char inArea[1024];
```

```
// receive message from the local sender
nBytes = Receive(&sender, inArea, 1024);
if (nBytes == -1)
  {
  printf("receive error-%s\n", whatsMyError());
  exit(-1);
  }

// get sender information
simplSetSenderParms(sender, senderInfo);

/*
    processing ...
*/

// been away doing other things; is "sender" still awaiting a reply?
if (simplCheckProcess(&senderInfo) == -1)
  {
  // sender has gone, no need to send a reply
  exit(0);
  }
}
```

void simplCheckProcess(SIMPL_REC *rec)

Description: The simplCheckProcess() function checks to see whether a process is still alive. It returns a 0 if the process is alive and a -1 if not.

Example: See the example in simplSetSenderParms().

int returnProxy(int proxyNumber)

Description: The returnProxy() function returns the true value of a proxy just received by a Receive() call. proxyNumber is the value $\leq$ -2 returned by the instance of the Receive() call. The proxy number returned will be $\geq$ 1. This curious arrangement arises due to the fact that the return value of the Receive() function is $\geq$ 0 for messages, null or otherwise. Failures are indicated by -1. This leaves only values $\leq$ -1 if we want to keep Receive() as a simple integer function. Accordingly, when a sender uses Trigger() to send a proxy with a of value 7 say (recall that proxies must be an integer 0), the Trigger() function sends it to the receiver as -7. The Receive() function will then return a value of -8. Plugging this value into returnProxy() returns 7, the value of the original proxy.

Example: This example shows the mechanics of a proxy sender and a proxy receiver. The sender sends a proxy equal to 1.

```c
#include <simpl.h>

void sender()
{
int proxy = 1;
int receiverId;

// SIMPL name attach
name_attach("sender");
// name locate receiver process
receiverId = name_locate{"receiver");
// send the receiver the proxy
Trigger(receiverId, proxy);
}

void receiver()
{
int nBytes;
int proxy;
char inArea[1024];
char *sender;

// SIMPL name attach
name_attach("receiver");

// receive messages from senders
nBytes = Receive(&sender, inArea, 1024);
if (nBytes == -1)
  {
  printf("receive error-%s\n", whatsMyError());
  exit(-1);
  }
// is this a proxy?
if (nBytes < -1)
  {
  // get the value of the proxy
  proxy = returnProxy(nBytes);
  printf("proxy=%d\n", proxy);
  // printf will display "proxy=1"
  }
}
```

B.2   Python Language Functions

integer name_attach(string)

Description: See the description of name_attach() in the 'C' language section. The syntax is comparable with the 'C' function call.

Example: This script wants to SIMPL name attach the name "receiver".

```python
from simpl import name_attach
import sys
name = "receiver"

# SIMPL name attach
retVal = name_attach(name)
if retVal == -1:
    sys.exit(-1)
```

integer name_detach()

Description: See the description of name_detach() in the 'C' language section. The syntax is comparable to the 'C' function call.

Example: This script has name attached the name "receiver" and no longer requires SIMPL methods.

```python
import simpl
import sys
name = "receiver"

# SIMPL name attach
retVal = simpl.name_attach(name)
if retVal == -1:
    sys.exit(-1)
"""
        processing ...
"""
# detach name
simpl.name_detach()
```

integer sur_detach(integer)

Description: See the description of sur_detach() in the 'C' language section. The syntax is comparable to the 'C' function call.

Example: This script has name attached the name "sender" and has name located a process called "receiver" on a remote host called "remote_host". It no longer requires the connection for whatever reason.

```python
import simpl
import sys
myName = "sender"
name = "remote_host:receiver"

# SIMPL name attach
retVal = simpl.name_attach(myName)
if retVal == -1:
    sys.exit(-1)
# name locate remote process
remoteId = name_locate(name)
if remoteId == -1:
    sys.exit(-1)
"""
        processing ...
"""
# no longer need a SIMPL connection to this remote process
simpl.sur_detach(remoteId)
```

integer name_locate(string)

Description: See the description of name_locate() in the 'C' language section. The syntax is comparable to the 'C' function call.

Example One: This script has name attached the name "sender" and wants to create a SIMPL connection to a local receiver called "receiver".

```python
import simpl
import sys
myName = "sender"
recvName = "receiver"

# SIMPL name attach
retVal = simpl.name_attach(myName)
if retVal == -1:
```

```
    sys.exit(-1)

# name locate "receiver"
receiverId = simpl.name_locate(recvName)
if receiverId == -1:
    sys.exit(-1)
"""
        processing ...
"""
```

Example Two: This script has name attached the name "sender" and wants to create a SIMPL connection to a remote receiver called "receiver" using the RS-232 protocol on host called "remoteHost".

```
import simpl
import sys
myName = "sender"
recvName = "RS232:remoteHost:receiver"

# SIMPL name attach
retVal = simpl.name_attach(myName)
if retVal == -1:
    sys.exit(-1)

# name locate "receiver"
receiverId = simpl.name_locate(recvName)
if receiverId == -1:
    sys.exit(-1)
"""
        processing ...
"""
```

---

tuple Receive()

Description: The Receive() function syntax for Python is somewhat different from its 'C' root function as the example below will show. Given that Python prefers to manage memory dynamically, instead of creating memory buffers and passing them to Receive(), the Python Receive() returns a tuple of values as they are set within the functionality. For more information see the description of Receive() in the 'C' language section.

Example One: This script has name attached the name "receiver" and then waits to receive messages from senders, then replying with a set number.

```
from simpl import *
from psimpl import *
import sys
inport struct

myName = "receiver"

# SIMPL name attach
retVal = name_attach(myName)
if retVal == -1:
  sys.exit(-1)

# receive a message
messageSize, senderId, message = Receive()

# check for error
if messageSize == -1:
  print "%s: receive error-%s" %(myName, whatsMyError())
  sys.exit(-1)
# is it a non-null message?
elif messageSize > 0:
  # extract the token from the message
  token = getBinaryValue(message, 0, SINT, "i")
  # react to the token
  """
        processing ...
  """
# reply to the sender
var = 7
out = struct.pack("i", var)
retVal = Reply(senderId, out)
if retVal == -1:
  print "%s: reply error-%s" %(myName, whatsMyError())
  sys.exit(-1)
```

Example Two: This script has name attached the name "receiver" and then waits to receive proxies from senders.

```
from simpl import *
from psimpl import *
import sys
inport struct

myName = "receiver"

# SIMPL name attach
retVal = name_attach(myName)
```

```
if  retVal == -1:
  sys.exit(-1)

# receive a message
messageSize, senderId, message = Receive()

# check for error
if messageSize == -1:
  print "%s: receive error-%s" %(myName, whatsMyError())
  sys.exit(-1)
# is it a proxy?
elif messageSize < -1:
  proxy = returnProxy(messageSize)
  # react to the proxy value
  """
        processing ...
  """
```

| integer Send(integer, BINARY, BINARY) |

Description: The Send() function syntax for Python is different from its 'C' root as the example below will show. For more information see the description of Send() in the 'C' language section.

Example: This script name attaches the name "sender" and then name locates a receiving process called "receiver". It then creates a message and sends it to "receiver" expecting a positive numerical reply. This sender example would work with the Receive() Example One above.

```
import sys
import struct
import simpl
import psimpl

# initialize some required variables
sName = "sender"
rName = "receiver"
in = struct.pack("i", 0)

# make a message to send
token = 10
var1 = 99
var2 = 999
var3 = 9999
out = struct.pack("iiii", token, var1, var2, var3)
```

```
# attach a simpl name
retVal = simpl.name_attach(sName)
if retVal == -1:
  print "%s: name attach error-%s" %(sName, simpl.whatsMyError())
  sys.exit(-1)

# name locate the receiver
receiverId = simpl.name_locate(rName)
if receiverId == -1:
  print "%s: name locate error-%s" %(sName, simpl.whatsMyError())
  sys.exit(-1)

# send message defined in "out" expecting a numerical reply in "in"
retVal = simpl.Send(receiverId, out, in)
if retVal == -1:
  print "%s: send error-%s" %(sName, simpl.whatsMyError())
  sys.exit(-1)

# extract the value of the message
var4 = getBinaryValue(in, 0, SINT, "i")
print "%s: in=%d" %(sName, var4)
```

integer Reply(integer, string/None)

Description: The Reply() function syntax for Python is comparable to the 'C'
function call. For more information see the description of Reply() in the 'C'
language section.

Example One: This script has name attached the name "receiver" and then
waits to receive messages from senders, then replying with "Thanks".

```
from simpl import *
import sys
inport struct

myName = "receiver"

# SIMPL name attach
retVal = name_attach(myName)
if retVal == -1:
  sys.exit(-1)

# receive a message
messageSize, senderId, message = Receive()
```

```
"""
        processing ...
"""
# reply to the sender
var = "Thanks"
out = struct.pack("s", var)
retVal = Reply(senderId, out)
if retVal == -1:
  print "%s: reply error-%s" %(myName, whatsMyError())
  sys.exit(-1)
```

Example Two: This script has name attached the name "receiver" and then waits to receive messages from senders, then replying with nothing.

```
from simpl import *
import sys

myName = "receiver"

# SIMPL name attach
retVal = name_attach(myName)
if retVal == -1:
  sys.exit(-1)

# receive a message
messageSize, senderId, message = Receive()
"""
        processing ...
"""
# reply to the sender)
retVal = Reply(senderId, None)
if retVal == -1:
  print "%s: reply error-%s" %(myName, whatsMyError())
  sys.exit(-1)
```

> **integer Trigger(integer)**

Description: The Trigger() function syntax for Python is comparable to the 'C' function call. For more information see the description of Trigger() in the 'C' language section.

Example: The following example demonstrates how a Python script sender Triggers a receiver. See Example Two in the Python Receive() function description above.

```
import simpl
import sys

# initialize some required variables
sName = "sender"
rName = "receiver"

# make a proxy value to send
proxy = 42

# attach a simpl name
retVal = simpl.name_attach(sName)
if retVal == -1:
    print "%s: name attach error-%s" %(sName, simpl.whatsMyError())
    sys.exit(-1)

# name locate the receiver
receiverId = simpl.name_locate(rName)
if receiverId == -1:
    print "%s: name locate error-%s" %(sName, simpl.whatsMyError())
    sys.exit(-1)

# generate a trigger
retVal = Trigger(receiverId, proxy)
if retVal == -1:
    print "%s: trigger error-%s" %(sName, simpl.whatsMyError())
    sys.exit(-1)
```

---

integer whatsMyRecvfd()

Description: The whatsMyRecvfd() function syntax for Python is comparable to the 'C' function call. For more information see the description of whatsMyRecvfd() in the 'C' language section. It is a very important function because it allows the Python program to be made aware of an incoming message while it is perhaps waiting for input from some other source.

Example: A good example can be taken from a Python script that puts up a Tk front end expecting user input. How does this program know to run a Receive() call in the case of an incoming message? See below.

```
import sys
from Tkinter import *
from simpl import *
```

```
# define functionality to be performed when a message is received
def hndlMessage(a, b):
  # receive a message
  messageSize, senderId, message = Receive()
  """
     process message ...
  """
  # reply to the sender
  retVal = Reply(senderId, None)
  if retVal == -1:
    print "%s: reply error-%s" %(rName, whatsMyError())
    sys.exit(-1)

# set this program's name
rName = "receiver"

# attach a simpl name
retVal = name_attach(rName)
if retVal == -1:
  print "%s: name attach error-%s" %(rName, whatsMyError())
  sys.exit(-1)

# get the receive FIFO file descriptor
fd = whatsMyRecvfd()

# initialize Tk for graphics
root = Tk()

# attach a callback for incoming simpl messages
root.tk.createfilehandler(fd, READABLE, hndlMessage)
  """
     build user interface ...
  """
# handle user input and simpl messaging
root.mainloop()
```

---

string whatsMyError()

Description: The whatsMyError() function syntax for Python is comparable to the 'C' function call. For more information see the description of whatsMyError() in the 'C' language section.

Example: A number of examples of its use are to be found in the preceding examples.

---
integer returnProxy(integer)

Description: The returnProxy() function syntax for Python is the same as the 'C' function call. For more information see the description of returnProxy() in the 'C' language section.

Example: See Example Two in the Python Receive() description above.

B.3   Tcl/Tk Language Procedures

| name_attach processName |

Description: The name_attach function is required by every process that expects
to send/receive messages to/from any other process. It is responsible for setting
up all of the SIMPL functionality that may be required. It must precede any
other Tcl/Tk SIMPL library calls. The string processName is the desired SIMPL
name of the process. This name must be unique on each host but not necessarily
on a network. A process that has successfully called this function is often referred
to as being 'name attached'. The length of processName is defined in the base
'C' SIMPL library.

The return code from name_attach depends on the Tcl/Tk package used. If
the 'C' shared library (fctclx.so) is used then the return code will be a string
containing, SIMPL_ID.process_ID. The shared library version of name_attach
returns a NULL string if the underlying SIMPL name_attach fails.

   If the fcgateway library package is used the return code will be the pid field in
the name_attach protocol message. As long as the tclSurrogate daemon process
is running this name_attach call should succeed.

Example: The calling process wants to attach the SIMPL name "SENDER"
using the fctclx shared library.

```
#!/usr/bin/wish

lappend auto_path $env(SIMPL_HOME)/lib
package require Fctclx

set myName SENDER

set myslot [name_attach $myName]
```

Example: The calling process wants to attach the SIMPL name "SENDER"
using the tclSurrogate libraries.

```
#!/usr/bin/wish

set gatewayAddr 127.0.0.1
set gatewayPort 8000
```

```
lappend auto_path $env(SIMPL_HOME)/lib
package require fcgateway
package require fcsocket

set myName SENDER

set mypid [name_attach $myName]
```

---

name_detach

Description: The name_detach function removes SIMPL related components from a program that has previously run a successful name_attach. This call should be made prior to exiting from the program. If the fctclx shared library is used this call will be made automatically by the SIMPL library. If the fcgateway/tclSurrogate library is used care must be taken to place the name_detach in the exit path.

Example: The calling process wants to detach the SIMPL name "SENDER" using the fctclx shared library.

```
#!/usr/bin/wish

lappend auto_path $env(SIMPL_HOME)/lib
package require Fctclx

set myName SENDER

set myslot [name_attach $myName]

... processing

name_detach
exit
```

Example: The calling process wants to detach the SIMPL name "SENDER" using the tclSurrogate libraries.

```
#!/usr/bin/wish

set gatewayAddr 127.0.0.1
set gatewayPort 8000
```

```
lappend auto_path $env(SIMPL_HOME)/lib
package require fcgateway
package require fcsocket

set myName SENDER

set mypid [name_attach $myName]

... processing

name_detach
exit
```

name_locate processName

Description: The name_locate function must be called prior to a Send or Trigger call to open the SIMPL communications channel to the intended receiver. If the fctclx shared library is used, then the SIMPL composite name string *name:protocolName:hostName:processName* is permitted as the argument. If the fcgateway library is used the straight processName is the only permitted form for the argument. The name_locate returns with the ID of the receiver process. A failure will return a 0 or -1 as the ID. (see 'C' library reference)

Example: This is an example of where the name of the process of interest is running on the local host.

```
...

set recvName BOBR
set recvID [name_locate $recvName]

...
```

Receive

Description: The Receive function receives messages from senders. If the fctclx shared library is used the message buffer size is fixed to 2k and is maintained internal to the shared library. The fcgateway library has a 64k maximum message size as the message field in the protocol is a two byte integer. In both cases the

Receive function will return a binary string containing: fromID numberbytes message. Failures are indicated by a -1 as the number of bytes.

Example: This is an example of a typical Receive call.

```
...

set buf [Receive]

binary scan $buf i1i1 fromWhom nbytes
binary scan $buf x8a$nbytes msg

... process msg
... build reply message (rMsg) of length rBytes

Reply $fromWhom $rMsg $rBytes
```

Send id outbuf outsize

Description: The Send function is a blocked send. This means that the calling program expects a reply from the receiver and waits until it gets one. The id is the result of a prior call to name_locate with regard to the receiver of interest. The outgoing message is contained in outbuf. The outgoing message size is outsize. The response to Send will be lead by an 8 byte header which can be interpreted as two integers. The first of these will be the internal slot used by the shared library for this message and the second will be the number of bytes contained in the response. In the event of an error the slot field will be set to -1.

Example: This is a typical Send call.

```
...

set rMsg [Send $targetID $sMsg $sBytes]

binary scan $rMsg i1i1a* slot rbytes rmsg

...
```

| Reply fromwhom replybuf replysize |

Description: The Reply function responds a return message from a receiver to a blocked sender indicated by the fromwhom channel. The reply message is contained in the replybuf and the size is replysize. Since it is difficult to intercept errors on TCP/IP sockets (the gateway version uses sockets) the Reply call will not return any error information.

Example: A typical Reply sequence.

```
set rMsg [binary format "s1a*" \
  $MYTOKEN(REGISTER)\
  $mypixel]

set rBytes [string length $rMsg]

Reply $fromWhom $rMsg $rBytes]

. . .
```

| Trigger id proxy |

Description: The Trigger function is currently only supported in the Tcl/Tk shared library. Trigger sends a proxy identified as an int to a receiving process identified by a prior call to name_locate() giving id. It is important that the proxy *MUST* be an integer > 0 AND $< 7\mathrm{FFFFFFF}$. This can thought of as a kick to the receiver and requires no reply. This function returns 0 on success and -1 for a failure. Failures can occur due to:
1. The calling process was never name attached,
2. Receiver does not exist,
3. Fifo errors, and
4. Proxy number is out of range.

Example: This process is triggering another local process called 'receiver'.

```
. . .

Trigger $targetID $myproxy

. . .
```

| logit traceloggerID file function mask logmask msg |

Description: The logit call interfaces into the SIMPL fclogger trace logger. This trace logger is denoted by the channel ID returned from a previous name_locate call. The file and function fields allow for identification as to where the trace log message originated. The mask bits interact with the logmask to determine if the message will be transmitted. The actual trace log message is contained in the msg field.

Example: A trace log call.

```
. . .

set logMask 0xff

set TRACE_MASK(MISC) 0x10

set this simplbook

. . .

set fn toggleX10

logit $loggerID $this $fn $TRACE_MASK(MISC) $logMask \
   [format "current temp=%d C limit=%d C" $mytemp $templimit]

. . .
```

B.4   Additional Notes

1. When errors are encountered, the 'C' variable int _simpl_errno (global to the library) is always set and the corresponding error string can be displayed by invoking whatsMyError(). This works in much the same way as errno and strerror(errno) do in 'C' language.

2. Most if not all internal warnings/errors are written to the file /var/tmp/simpl under Linux.

3. Macro definitions regarding maximal/minimal quantities such as MAX_PROGRAM_NAME_LEN are contained in $SIMPL_HOME/include/simplDefs.h.

4. With respect to Python functions, they are called as *simpl.function_call* in our examples. This is a good way because it reminds the programmer that the function has been called from the SIMPL module. The Python command *import simpl* precedes any such function call. If however the command *from simpl import* * is used, then the function call will be of the form *function_call* without the prefix allusion to simpl. See the examples in Python Language Functions for name_attach().

5. All Python SIMPL functions have been extended through calling 'C' SIMPL library functions. The ensuing Python SIMPL module is called simpl.

Appendix C

TCP/IP Surrogate - Details

In this appendix we address the operational details of the TCP/IP surrogate.

Operation

Suppose that we have the situation that a sender process exists on Host 1 and a receiver process exists on Host 2. The sender needs to send messages to the receiver and will use a TCP/IP connection. Let us examine the operation of the surrogates by following the numbers in Figure C.1.

1. The sender performs a **name_locate**("SIMPL_TCP:Host 2:receiver") call in order to make a connection to the remote receiver. During this function call a message is sent to the protocolRouter program inquiring as to whether a TCP/IP surrogate receiver (surrogate_r) is available for use. If so, the SIMPL name of this TCP/IP surrogate receiver is replied back to the sender.

2. surrogate_R then forks another TCP/IP surrogate_r in readiness for any forthcoming requests.

3. The sender **name_locate** call, now knowing the SIMPL name of its prospective surrogate receiver (surrogate_r) then sends a remote name locate message to surrogate_r.

4. surrogate_r then opens a TCP/IP socket to surrogate_S on Host 2. surrogate_r then sends a name locate message to surrogate_S. Upon receiving this message surrogate_S forks a surrogate_s child which completes the surrogate socket pair, viz. surrogate_r/surrogate_s. Upon a successful fork,

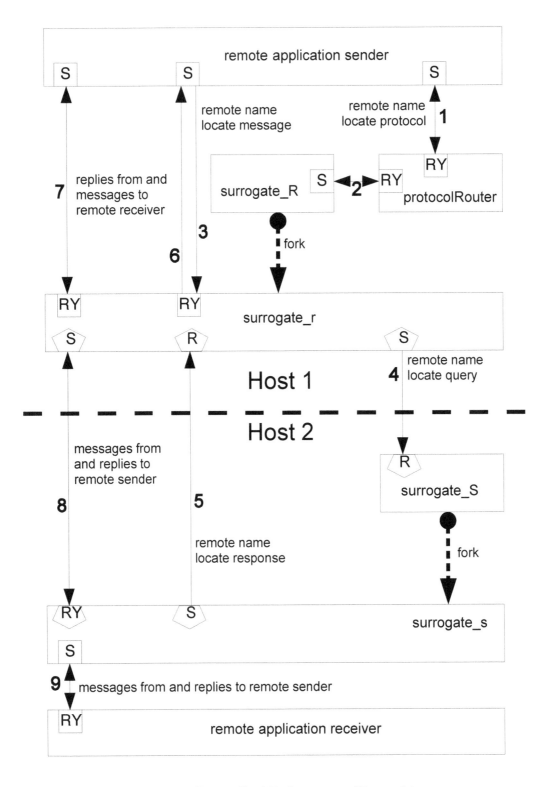

Figure C.1: TCP/IP Surrogate Networking

surrogate_s then has the original name locate message of its parent surrogate_S. surrogate_s then performs a local name locate on the receiver process.

5. surrogate_s replies back to the surrogate_r the result of the name locate.

6. surrogate_r replies back to the result of the remote name locate for the receiver process. **IMPORTANT** Steps 1-6 above are all contained within the original *name_locate*("Host 2:SIMPL_TCP:receiver") call made by the sender. This is what *lies under the hood*.

7. The sender sends messages to and receives replies from the surrogate receiver, surrogate_r. As far as the sender is concerned, it is the remote receiver that it is in contact with.

8. The surrogate receiver, surrogate_r and the surrogate sender surrogate_s, exchange messages and replies.

9. The surrogate sender, surrogate_s, sends messages to the receiver program and receives replies in return. As far as the receiver program is concerned it is in direct contact with the sender.

For a complete description of the tokenized messages internal to the surrogates see Appendix F.

Starting Up

The first thing that is required when running surrogate programs is the presence of the protocol router program. For details on the protocol router, see Section 7.3. It is started and run in the background as follows: **protocolRouter &**

The next thing is to start the TCP/IP surrogate program: surrogateTcp. It can be started and run in the background as follows: **surrogateTcp &**. This program has a number of command line arguments defined as follows:

-a The A port used to bind sockets to; defaults to 8001.

-b The B port used to bind sockets to; defaults to A port.

-i The width of an integer, 4 bytes for a 32-bit integer, 8 bytes for a 64-bit integer; defaults to 4 bytes.

-k The value of the keep alive time out in seconds; defaults to 10. A value of 0 indicates no keep alive is to be run.

-n The value of a name locate time out in seconds; defaults to 60. This is the
   allowable time taken for a remote name locate call before timing out and
   returning a failure.

Example One: surrogateTcp -k0 -n120 &
This example turns off the keep alive mechanism and increases the name locate
time out to two minutes on what is perhaps a slow network.

Example Two: surrogateTcp -a8020 -k60 &
This example changes the port to 8020, perhaps due to a port confliction with
some other device and slows down the keep alive to once per minute.

Appendix D

RS-232 Surrogate - Details

In this appendix we address the operational details of the RS-232 surrogate.

D.1   Operation

Suppose again as in the Appendix C on TCP/IP surrogates that we have the situation that a sender process exists on Host 1 and a receiver process exists on Host 2. The sender needs to send messages to the receiver via an RS-232 connection. Let us examine the operation of the surrogates by following the numbers in Figure D.1.

1. The sender performs a *name_locate*("Host2:SIMPL_RS232:receiver") call in order to make a connection to the remote receiver. During this call a message is sent to the protocolRouter program inquiring as to whether a TCP/IP surrogate receiver (surrogate_r) is available for use. If so, the SIMPL name of this TCP/IP surrogate receiver is replied back to the sender.

2. surrogate_R then forks another TCP/IP surrogate_r in readiness for any forthcoming requests.

3. The sender *name_locate* call, now knowing the SIMPL name of its prospective surrogate receiver (surrogate_r) then sends a remote name locate message to surrogate_r.

4a. surrogate_r then sends the remote name locate message to the program called rs232_rw. This program reads from and writes to the serial port.

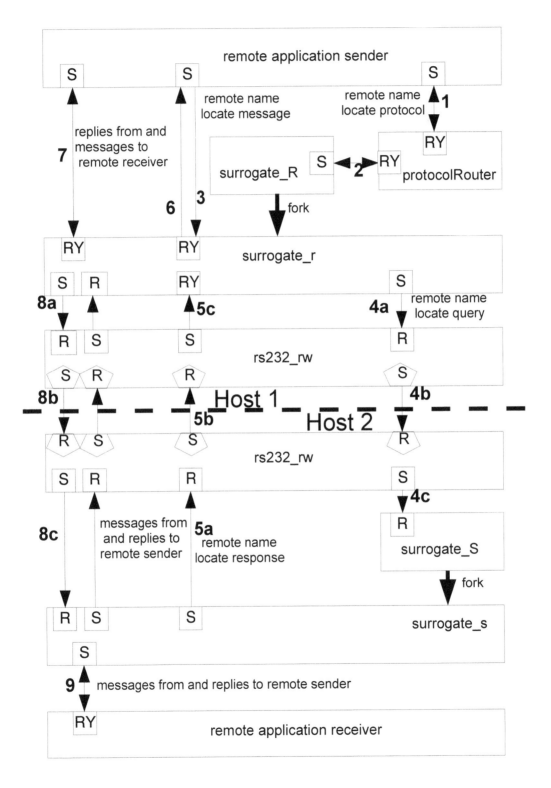

Figure D.1: RS-232 Surrogate Networking

4b. rs232_rw then writes the remote name locate message out the serial port where the message is then read by its counterpart on Host 2.

4c. rs232_rw having received the remote name locate message then sends the message on to surrogate_S. Upon receiving this message surrogate_S forks a surrogate_s child which completes the surrogate socket pair, viz. surrogate_r/surrogate_s. Upon a successful fork, surrogate_s then has the original name locate message of its parent surrogate_S. surrogate_s then performs a local name locate on the receiver process.

5a. surrogate_s replies the results of the name locate back to rs232_rw.

5b. rs232_rw then writes this result out the serial line to its counterpart on Host 1.

5c. Upon receiving the result of the name locate message from rs232_rw on Host 2, rs232_rw on Host1 then forwards the message on to surrogate_r.

6. surrogate_r replies back the result of the remote name locate for the remote receiver process. **IMPORTANT:** Steps 1-6 above are all contained within the original name_locate("Host 2:SIMPL_RS232:receiver") call made by the sender. This is *what lies under the hood*.

7. The sender sends messages to and receives replies from the surrogate receiver, surrogate_r. As far as the sender is concerned, it is the remote receiver that it is in contact with.

8. The surrogate receiver, surrogate_r, rs232_rw on Host 1, and rs232_rw on Host 2 and the surrogate sender surrogate_s exchange messages and replies.

9. The surrogate sender surrogate_s, sends messages to the receiver program and receives replies in return. As far as the receiver program is concerned it is in direct contact with the sender.

D.2 Starting Up

As in the section on the TCP/IP surrogates, the first thing that is required when running surrogate programs is the presence of the protocol router program. For details on the protocol router, see Section 7.3. It is started and run in the background as follows: **protocolRouter &**.

Furthermore, the rs232_rw program must also be started. It is started and run in the background as follows: **rs232_rw &**. This program has a number of command line arguments defined as follows:

-i: the width of an integer, 4 bytes for a 32-bit integer, 8 bytes for a 64-bit integer; defaults to 4 bytes.

-s: the name of the serial device to be used. The default value is /dev/ttyS0.

-v: the boolean value of the verbosity. It defaults to 0 which is off. The verbosity prints to stdout the sorts of messages that are being read off or written to the serial port.

IMPORTANT: Note that it is NOT the responsibility of SIMPL to set the appropriate serial port values. There are a number of ways and utility programs to do this depending on the operating system. The default port opening values etc. can be found in a file called rs232.h in the SIMPL development tree.

Example: rs232_rw -s/dev/ttyS1 -v &
This example sets the serial port to /dev/ttyS1 and turns on the verbosity.

The next thing is to start the RS-232 surrogate program: surrogateRS232. It can be started and run in the background as follows: **surrogateRS232 &**. This program has a number of command line arguments defined as follows:

-i: the width of an integer, 4 bytes for a 32-bit integer, 8 bytes for a 64-bit integer; defaults to 4 bytes.

-k: the value of the keep alive time out in seconds; defaults to 10. A value of 0 indicates no keep alive.

-n: the value of a name locate time out in seconds; defaults to 60. This is the allowable time taken for a remote name locate call before timing out and returning a failure.

Example: surrogateRS232 -k0 -n120 &
This example turns off the keep alive mechanism and increases the name locate time out to two minutes on what is perhaps a slow network.

Appendix E

tclSurrogate Protocol

The so-called tclSurrogate protocol is so named because it was first used to connect a Tcl applet to the SIMPL framework. Since that time the embedded protocol has been used in many other instances than Tcl applets (Tcl/Tk Windows -> SIMPL, VB Windows -> SIMPL, IO Anywhere network appliance -> SIMPL).

The concept of the tclSurrogate is really very straightward. The tclSurrogate parent is started up and listens for connections on a predefined TCP/IP port. (default to port 8000). When a connection is made and accepted the tclSurrogate forks a child process whose purpose is to act as the SIMPL interface to the rest of the SIMPL application. The process making the connection and this child communicate with each other over the TCP/IP socket which exists between them. The structures they use to communicate on this socket is what we are terming the tclSurrogate protocol.

E.1   General Message Format

The basic protocol message format is as follows:

token(2)	nbytes(2)	ID(4) data(token dependant)

where the number in brackets represents the size of the field in bytes.

E.2   Some Terminology

We also need to decide on some naming conventions for the various elements
involved in a message pass via the tclSurrogate child process.

There are basically three players that are involved:

- socket connected app (**sockapp**)

- tclSurrogate child (**child**)

- SIMPL sender or receiver (**SIMPL sender or receiver**)

When illustrating the protocol in detail below we will be using these short
hand forms for these players.

E.3   Tokens

The following tokens form the basis of this protocol. The master source for this
information is in the 'C' header located at **$SIMPL_HOME/tcl/include/surroMsgs.h**

Token	Value
NAME_ATTACH	0
NAME_DETACH	1
NAME_LOCATE	2
SEND	3
REPLY	4
RELAY	5
IS_LOGGER_UP	6
LOGIT	7
SEND_NO_REPLY	8
ACK	9
PING	10

E.4   NAME_ATTACH

sockapp -> child

0	32	n/a(4)	SIMPL name(20)	n/a(4)	n/a(4)

child -> sockapp

| 4 | 32 | -1 | SIMPL name(20) | pid(4) | slot(4) |

When the sockapp issues the NAME_ATTACH message it has the effect of setting the SIMPL name on the child process.

E.5 NAME_DETACH

sockapp -> child

| 1 | 0 |

child -> sockapp

| 4 | 4 | -1 |

The NAME_DETACH causes the child process to exit after a 2 second delay.

E.6 NAME_LOCATE

sockapp -> child

| 2 | 28 | n/a(4) | SIMPL name(20) | n/a(4) |

child -> sockapp

| 4 | 28 | -1 | SIMPL name(20) | rc(4) |

The NAME_LOCATE will have the effect of performing a local *name_locate* for the SIMPL name. The rc field will contain the result of that call.

E.7 SEND

sockapp -> child

| 3 | 4+sbytes | toWhom(4) | sdata(sbytes) |

child -> SIMPL receiver(toWhom)

| sdata(sbytes) |

SIMPL receiver -> child

| rdata(rbytes) |

child -> sockapp

| 4 | 4+rbytes | -1 | rdata(rbytes) |

E.8 REPLY

The use of this token has been detailed in the other paragraphs.

E.9 RELAY

SIMPL sender(fromWhom) -> child

| sdata(sbytes) |

child -> sockapp

| 5 | 4+sbytes | fromWhom(4) | sdata(sbytes) |

sockapp -> child

| 4 | 4+rbytes | fromWhom(4) | rdata(rbytes) |

child -> SIMPL sender(fromWhom)

| rdata(rbytes) |

E.10 IS_LOGGER_UP

sockapp -> child

| 6 | 28 | n/a(4) | trace logger name(20) | n/a(4) |

child -> sockapp

| 4 | 28 | -1 | trace logger name(20) | loggerID(4) |

NOTE: the trace logger name isn't currently checked in the child code, so this call will return the global loggerID variable for the tclSurrogate parent's trace logger irrespective of the supplied trace logger name.

E.11 LOGIT

sockapp -> child

| 7 | 52+msglen | loggerID(4) | fileName(20) | funcName20) | mask(4) | globalMask(4) |

There is no response to the LOGIT call.

E.12   SEND_NO_REPLY

sockapp -> child

| 8 | 4+sbytes | toWhom(4) | sdata(sbytes) |

child -> SIMPL receiver(toWhom)

| sdata(sbytes) |

The **Reply** from the SIMPL receiver is simply discarded in this instance.

E.13   ACK

sockapp -> child

| 9 |

The ACK is not responded to.

E.14   PING

sockapp -> child

| 10 |

child -> sockapp

| 4 | 4 | -1 |

Appendix F

Surrogate Internal Messages

SIMPL surrogates communicate with each other via tokenized message passing. See Chapter 5 for a detailed description of tokenized message passing. Table F.1 contains a list of the various tokens that are used.

The following is a list of the more important tokens, what they mean and where they are used.

SUR_NAME_LOCATE This token starts out in a remote name locate call. It then goes to the relevant surrogate_r program. From there it goes to the surrogate_S program on the remote host. This causes surrogate_S to fork a surrogate_s program which then carries out a local name locate for the desired receiver process.

SUR_SEND This token originates in surrogate_r. By setting this token surrogate_r is telling its surrogate_s partner that a sender-originated message is following.

SUR_REPLY This is the message token sent from surrogate_s to its partner surrogate_r implying that the following message is a reply to the previously sent message.

SUR_CLOSE If a surrogate_r gets a proxy to shutdown from its local sender or if surrogate_r detects that the sender has disappeared then it sends a message with this token set to its surrogate_s partner. If the sender has terminated, then neither of the surrogates are required and this tokenized message tells surrogate_s to exit.

SUR_PROXY This token originates in surrogate_r. By setting this token surrogate_r is telling its surrogate_s partner that a sender originated proxy is

Token	Value	Purpose
SUR_NAME_ATTACH	0	deprecated
SUR_NAME_DETACH	1	deprecated
SUR_NAME_LOCATE	2	name locate requests
SUR_SEND	3	send message
SUR_REPLY	4	reply message
SUR_CLOSE	5	surrogate quit
SUR_PROXY	6	proxy message
SUR_ERROR	7	error message
SUR_ALIVE	8	keep alive message
SUR_ALIVE_REPLY	9	keep alive reply message
SUR_SURROGATE_READY	10	message to protocol router
SUR_REQUEST_PROTOCOL	11	message to protocol router
SUR_DUMP_TABLE	12	message to protocol router

Table F.1: Surrogate Tokens

following.

SUR_ERROR This token originates in surrogate_s. By setting this token surrogate_s is telling its surrogate_r partner that some sort of problem has occurred.

SUR_ALIVE Both surrogate_r and surrogate_s send this message token to each other as a keep alive inquiry.

SUR_ALIVE_REPLY Both surrogate_r and surrogate_s send this message token to each other as a response to a keep alive inquiry.

SUR_SURROGATE_READY This token represents a message from surrogate_R to the protocol router stating that a new surrogate_r is ready for use.

SUR_REQUEST_PROTOCOL This message type originates in a remote name locate call whereby a message is sent to the protocol router asking for the SIMPL name of an available surrogate_r of the desired protocol.

SUR_DUMP_TABLE This message type is sent by the utility program called *dumpProtocolTable* to the protocol router. This message causes the protocol router to reply the contents of its internal surrogate_r table which the *dumpProtocolTable* program displays to stdout.

Appendix G

Trace Logger

Tracking down anomalies in executing code is a subject for a book on its own. Source code debuggers have their place as do strategically placed temporary printf()s. However, both are highly intrusive to the executable itself.

The source code debuggers require that the code be compiled in a specific way. The compiler adds special code into the executable to allow that executable to be put under the control of another program: the debugger. This allows the programmer to set break points, step through code, examine variables etc.

For quick checking of program flow or variable contents, strategically placed printf()s are often used. However, this requires that the executable be modified at the source level and then recompiled before testing. Most often those printf()s need to be removed before the executable undergoes final testing and is deployed.

Neither of these debugging techniques is useful for doing any trouble shooting on a deployed executable already in the field. For this we need a trace logger. The ideal trace logger would:

- Minimally impact the executable performance thereby allowing trace logger calls to be liberally sprinkled throughout production code.

- Allow for verbosity of the trace log output to be altered on a running executable.

- Allow for multiple levels of information to be individually enabled or disabled.

The SIMPL core toolkit comes with a very capable trace logger which for historical reasons is called **fclogger**.

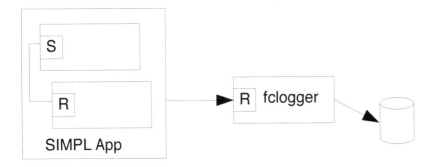

Figure G.1: Trace Logger

This trace logger comes in two parts:

- A very basic SIMPL receiver which receives a text message and redirects that to the standard output.

- A simpllog API which *hides* the sending half behind a *printf-like* API call.

```
fcLogx(char *filename,
char *function,
unsigned int globalMask,
unsigned int userMask,
char *format,
... )
```

where

filename - user supplied name of file (often just __FILE__)

function - user supplied name of local function

globalMask - 32 bit mask which allows for 32 separate logging "levels" to be enabled/disabled across the application

userMask - 32 bit mask indicating which mask level(s) apply to this particular call

format - full printf style format

... - full printf style variable list

The idea is that you substitute the fcLogx() call in your code wherever you would normally have put a printf for debugging and/or error display. The userMask bit is set on each fcLogx() call by the programmer when the source code is written. The globalMask bits are set by any combination of:

- default global variable

- command line override

- special SIMPL message for mask override

Only messages where the globalMask and userMask bits are both set are transmitted to the trace logger. Otherwise the fcLogx() simply returns immediately after the mask comparison.[1]

The **fclogger** is a very basic SIMPL receiver. When it receives a message it simply dumps the entire contents of that message out to the console screen (stdout) and sends back a NULL Reply.

Of course it is a simple matter of redirecting that output to get it to appear inside a file. In chapter 8 we show an example of the trace logger output being redirected to a file.

This SIMPL trace logger is a very powerful tool. Through its use one can provide very powerful feedback about the inner workings of the code in ways that are much less intrusive than a source code debugger. Furthermore, you can leave your trace debugging statements in your code without incurring an appreciable performance penalty.

In chapter 8 we illustrated the creation of test0001. Watch what happens when we make a very basic change to our test0001 script to add another command line argument to the stimulator invocation line.

```
stimulator -n BOBS -r BOBR -m 0x0 -l LOGGER -b &
```

The addition of the -m argument has stopped the flow of log messages to the trace log file. We didn't have to do any recompilation to get this!

With the tokenized SIMPL messaging into the receiver it would be a simple exercise to design a message would allow you to alter the trace log mask while the receiver was running. In other words, we could suppress or enable the flow of log messages on the fly without stopping and restarting the SIMPL modules.

---

[1]For examples of the SIMPL trace logger in action you can consult any of the softwareICs which are fully fclogger enabled.

Appendix H

Warning and Error Messages

Code	Description
1	No SIMPL name provided for name attach.
2	No fifo path environment variable defined.
3	SIMPL name is probably in use.
4	Unable to create shmem for message communication.
5	Unable to delete shmem from message communication.
6	Unable to attach shmem created for message communication.
7	Unable to detach shmem created for message communication.
8	Unable to remove shmem created for message communication.
9	No SIMPL name has been attached to this process.
10	Error in creating trigger fifo.
11	Error in getting trigger fifo.
12	Error in opening trigger fifo.
13	Error in reading from trigger fifo.
14	Error in writing to trigger fifo.
15	Bad fifo file descriptor.
16	Unable to find the surrogate process.
17	Unable to ascertain current host name.
18	Unable to locate remote process.
19	Received message exceeds receiver buffer allocation.
20	Reply message exceeds sender buffer allocation.
21	Receive/Reply problem ... could be a failed receiver.
22	Requested name too short.
23	Too many colons in requested name locate.

continued on next page

Code	Description
24	No system host name set.
25	System host name is too long.
26	Protocol not in router table.
27	No more room in remote receiver table.
28	Unable to open fifo directory.
29	Command line args parsing error.
30	Proxy value must be >= 1.
31	Local host has no available IP information.

Table H.1: Warning and Error Messages

Appendix I

SIMPL License

The SIMPL project essentially uses two licenses:

- the Lesser General Public License (LGPL)

- the Public Domain License

The details of these licenses are available for your perusal in the $SIMPL_HOME/license subdirectory.

We want as many people to use SIMPL as possible. We don't want to restrict its usage in commercial custom software in any way. However, we expect SIMPL users to respect the licenses under which different parts of the SIMPL toolset were released.

There is a legal angle to these licenses and we'll defer those debates to better qualified individuals. It is more important that SIMPL users understand the spirit of these licenses as we interpret them.

The SIMPL core library is for example, licensed under the LGPL. The LGPL license essentially says that since we own the copyright to the SIMPL core code we can dictate the terms of usage. The LGPL gives SIMPL core code users generous terms of usage which include full and unfettered access to the source code. The only stipulation that the LGPL insists upon is that if you choose to make changes to the SIMPL core and redistribute those, then you cannot change the terms of the access that we originally gave to you. When stated in this way this seems like a fair bargain.

In practical terms this means that if any user (including commercial custom software vendors) makes changes to the SIMPL core and then redistributes those changes with their application, they cannot restrict access to those changes. We would hope that in those instances the users would do the honourable thing and recontribute their changes back to the SIMPL project without having to be asked. These terms however, do not extend to the user SIMPL application itself. The code to that portion of a custom application can remain proprietary. We don't make any distinction if the SIMPL application is statically or dynamically linked to the SIMPL core libraries.

The Public Domain sections which include the SIMPL softwareICs, were given freely to users without any conditions. We would encourage users who improve upon the code under this license to contribute back to the SIMPL project but there is no legal obligation to do so.

Glossary

API - Application Program Interface.

CPU - Central Processing Unit.

FIFO - First In First Out; a named pipe.

IC - Integrated Circuit.

ID - IDentification.

IP - Internet Protocol.

IPC - InterProcess Communication.

GNU - GNU's Not Unix.

LGPL - Lesser General Public License Agreement.

OOP - Object Oriented Programming.

OS - Operating System.

PC - Personal Computer.

PID - Process IDentification.

QA - Quality Assurance.

receiver - A process which receives SIMPL messages.

RTOS - Real Time Operating System.

sender - A process which sends SIMPL messages.

SIMPL - Synchronous Interprocess Message Project for Linux.

SIMPL ID - A unique integer representing a receiver which is returned by a *name_locate* library function call and used by a sender to direct messages to said receiver

SIMPL System - a collection of two or more processes that use SIMPL to communicate messages to each other.

SIPC - Synchronous InterProcess Communication.

SRY - Send/Receive/Reply.

STF - SIMPL Testing Framework.

surrogate - A SIMPL process that uses a given protocol for communications between a sender and a receiver which reside on different host machines.

TCP - Transmission Control Protocol.

TCP/IP - Transmission Control Protocol/Internet Protocol.
UI - User Interface.
XML - EXtensible Markup Language.

Index

www.ingramcontent.com/pod-product-compliance
Lightning Source LLC
Chambersburg PA
CBHW060521060326
40690CB00017B/3340